The Art of Understanding Your Daughter: a Parent's Guide

Mokhtari Behzad

Published by Mokhtari Behzad, 2024.

THE ART OF UNDERSTANDING YOUR DAUGHTER: A PARENT'S GUIDE

First edition. April 2, 2024.

Copyright © 2024 Mokhtari Behzad.

ISBN: 979-8223491231

Written by Mokhtari Behzad.

Table of Contents

Chapter 1: Introduction

- BUILDING A STRONG Parent-Daughter Relationship

Building a strong parent-daughter relationship is crucial for the emotional well-being and development of both individuals. In today's fast-paced world, where work and other commitments often take precedence, it can be easy for parents and daughters to drift apart. However, making a conscious effort to strengthen this bond can have numerous benefits for both parties. Research has shown that girls who have a strong relationship with their parents are more likely to have higher self-esteem, better academic performance, and improved mental health.

One of the key aspects of building a strong parent-daughter relationship is communication. Open and honest communication is essential for fostering trust and understanding between parents and daughters. This means creating a safe space where both parties feel comfortable expressing their thoughts, feelings, and concerns. It is important for parents to listen actively to their daughters and show empathy towards their experiences. By listening attentively and without judgment, parents can better understand their daughters' perspectives and feelings, which can help strengthen the bond between them.

Another important aspect of building a strong parent-daughter relationship is spending quality time together. In today's fast-paced world, it can be challenging to find time to bond with your daughter amidst work, school, and other commitments. However, making an effort to prioritize quality time together can have a significant impact on the parent-daughter relationship. This can involve doing activities together that both parties enjoy, such as going for a hike, watching a movie, or cooking a meal together. By spending quality time together, parents and daughters can create lasting memories and strengthen their connection.

In addition to communication and quality time together, it is important for parents to be supportive and provide guidance to their daughters. Adolescence can be a challenging time for girls, as they navigate the complexities of school, relationships, and identity. Parents can support their daughters by being a source of encouragement and guidance. This can involve offering advice, helping to problem-solve, and providing emotional support during difficult times. By being a supportive and involved parent, you can help your daughter navigate the challenges of adolescence and build a strong foundation for a healthy parent-daughter relationship.

It is also important for parents to set boundaries and expectations with their daughters. Boundaries are important for establishing a sense of structure and respect within the parent-daughter relationship. This can involve setting limits on behavior, enforcing rules, and communicating expectations clearly. By setting boundaries, parents can help their daughters understand what is acceptable and what is not, which can help prevent conflicts and misunderstandings. Additionally, setting boundaries can help parents and daughters develop a sense of mutual respect and understanding within the relationship.

Lastly, building a strong parent-daughter relationship also involves recognizing and celebrating your daughter's achievements and successes. It is important for parents to acknowledge and praise their daughters for their accomplishments, whether big or small. By celebrating your daughter's successes, you can boost her self-esteem, confidence, and motivation. This can help foster a positive and supportive parent-daughter relationship, where both parties feel appreciated and valued. By recognizing and celebrating your daughter's achievements, you can strengthen the bond between you and create a positive and nurturing environment for her growth and development. By focusing on communication, spending quality time together, providing support and guidance, setting boundaries, and celebrating achievements, parents can help strengthen the bond with their daughters. A strong parent-daughter relationship can have numerous benefits for both parties, including higher self-esteem, improved academic performance, and better mental health. By making a conscious effort to prioritize and nurture this relationship, parents can help their daughters thrive and succeed in all aspects of their lives.

- Understanding the Unique Challenges of Raising a Daughter

Raising a daughter can be a rewarding and fulfilling experience for parents, but it also comes with its own set of unique challenges. In today's society, girls face a myriad of pressures and expectations that can impact their self-esteem, confidence, and overall well-being. As parents, it is important to understand these challenges in order to provide the necessary support and guidance to help our daughters navigate through them successfully.

One of the key challenges that girls face is the pressure to conform to societal standards of beauty and perfection. From a young age, girls are bombarded with images in the media that promote unrealistic ideals of beauty and body image. This can lead to low self-esteem, body dissatisfaction, and even disordered eating behaviors. As parents, it is important to foster a positive body image in our daughters by promoting self-acceptance, focusing on health and well-being rather than appearance, and teaching them to value their unique qualities and strengths.

Another challenge that girls face is the pressure to excel academically and professionally. While girls have made significant strides in education and the workforce in recent years, they still face gender discrimination and bias that can impact their opportunities for success. As parents, it is important to support and empower our daughters to pursue their passions and interests, regardless of societal expectations or stereotypes. Encouraging them to challenge themselves, develop their skills and talents, and strive for academic and career success can help them overcome these obstacles and reach their full potential.

Additionally, girls may also face challenges in their relationships with peers, romantic partners, and family members. The pressure to fit in and be accepted by others can lead to feelings of insecurity, loneliness, and peer pressure. As parents, it is important to teach our daughters how to establish healthy boundaries, communicate effectively, and cultivate positive relationships with others. Encouraging them to be assertive, confident, and kind can help them navigate through the ups and downs of friendships, dating, and family dynamics with grace and resilience.

Furthermore, girls may also struggle with issues related to mental health, such as anxiety, depression, and stress. The pressures and demands of modern society can take a toll on their emotional well-being, leading to feelings of overwhelm, sadness, and hopelessness. As parents, it is important to be attuned to our daughters' emotional needs and provide them with the necessary support, resources, and coping strategies to manage their mental health effectively. Encouraging open and honest communication, seeking professional help when needed, and modeling healthy self-care practices can help our daughters build resilience and maintain their emotional well-being. By empowering our daughters with the tools, resources, and guidance they need to navigate through these challenges successfully, we can help them develop into confident, resilient, and empowered young women who are capable of overcoming obstacles and achieving their dreams. It is essential for parents to cultivate a supportive and nurturing environment that fosters their daughters' growth, self-discovery, and self-expression, while also encouraging them to embrace their uniqueness and individuality. By providing unwavering love, encouragement, and guidance, we can help our daughters thrive and flourish in all aspects of their lives.

Chapter 2: The Developmental Stages of Girls

- INFANCY AND TODDLER Years

Infancy and toddler years are crucial stages in a child's development that lay the foundation for all future growth and learning. During infancy, which typically spans from birth to around two years of age, babies undergo rapid physical, cognitive, and emotional changes. Infants develop their motor skills, learn to communicate, and form attachments with their caregivers. This stage is a period of incredible growth and vulnerability, as infants rely entirely on adults for their care and protection.

One of the key milestones during infancy is the development of attachment, which is the emotional bond that forms between an infant and their primary caregiver. This attachment provides a sense of security and lays the groundwork for future relationships and emotional well-being. Babies who form secure attachments with their caregivers are more likely to develop healthy relationships later in life and have better emotional regulation skills.

As infants grow and transition into the toddler years, typically defined as ages two to three, they become more independent and curious about the world around them. Toddlers are known for their boundless energy and newfound abilities, such as walking, talking, and problem-solving. This stage is marked by significant cognitive growth, as toddlers begin to explore their environment, acquire language skills, and develop a sense of self.

During the toddler years, children also start to assert their autonomy and test boundaries, which can sometimes lead to challenging behavior. Tantrums, resistance to authority, and defiance are common during this stage as toddlers navigate their growing independence and developing sense of identity. It is important for caregivers to provide a balance of support and guidance to help toddlers navigate this stage of development successfully.

Parenting during the infancy and toddler years can be both rewarding and challenging. It is important for caregivers to provide a nurturing and responsive environment that supports the child's development. This includes fostering secure attachment relationships, providing opportunities for exploration and learning, and setting appropriate boundaries and limits. Caregivers should also prioritize the child's physical and emotional well-being, ensuring that their needs for food, sleep, and affection are met consistently.

In addition to the importance of caregiver interactions, the physical environment also plays a significant role in infant and toddler development. Creating a safe, stimulating, and nurturing environment can help support children's growth and learning. Providing age-appropriate toys, engaging in interactive play, and establishing routines can all contribute to a child's development during these formative years.

Early childhood education and childcare programs also play a crucial role in supporting children's development during the infancy and toddler years. High-quality early childhood education can provide infants and toddlers with opportunities for social interaction, cognitive stimulation, and emotional support. These programs can help foster positive relationships with peers and caregivers, promote language development, and facilitate the acquisition of important skills. Caregivers play a central role in supporting children's development during this stage, providing a nurturing and stimulating environment that promotes secure attachment relationships, cognitive growth, and emotional well-being. By understanding the unique needs and characteristics of infants and toddlers, caregivers can support their development in a holistic and responsive manner. Through appropriate caregiving, environmental support, and early education opportunities, children can thrive during these formative years and build a strong foundation for future success.

- Childhood and Adolescence

Childhood and adolescence are two critical stages of human development that shape the trajectory of an individual's life. These stages are characterized by significant physical, cognitive, emotional, and social changes that lay the foundation for future growth and success. Understanding the complexities of childhood and adolescence is essential for parents, educators, and policymakers to support young people in reaching their full potential.

Childhood is the period from infancy to adolescence, typically defined as the first 12 years of life. During this stage, rapid physical growth and development occur, as children learn to walk, talk, and interact with their environment. Cognitive abilities also undergo significant advancements, with children developing language, problem-solving skills, and abstract thinking. Emotional development in childhood is marked by the formation of attachments, the development of self-awareness, and the emergence of basic emotions like joy, sadness, and fear. Socially, children begin to form relationships with peers and adults, learning important social skills such as sharing, empathy, and cooperation.

Adolescence, on the other hand, is the transitional period between childhood and adulthood, spanning from approximately ages 12 to 18. This stage is characterized by rapid physical changes, as the body undergoes puberty and reaches sexual maturity. Cognitive development in adolescence is marked by increased abstract thinking, self-reflection, and the ability to consider multiple perspectives. Emotionally, adolescents experience intense feelings and mood swings as they navigate the challenges of identity formation and autonomy. Socially, adolescence is a time of increasing independence from parents and reliance on peers for support and validation.

Both childhood and adolescence are influenced by a myriad of factors, including genetics, environment, culture, and socio-economic status. Understanding the interplay of these influences is critical for supporting young people in their development. Parents play a key role in providing a nurturing and stable environment for children to thrive, offering love, support, and guidance as they navigate the challenges of growing up. Educators also play a crucial role in shaping the development of children and adolescents, providing opportunities for learning, growth, and self-discovery in a safe and supportive setting.

At the policy level, governments and organizations must prioritize investments in programs and services that support the healthy development of children and adolescents. This includes access to quality education, healthcare, mental health services, and social support systems that address the unique needs of young people. By investing in the well-being of children and adolescents, we can ensure that future generations have the resources and support they need to succeed in life. Understanding the complexities of these stages is essential for parents, educators, and policymakers to support young people in reaching their full potential. By investing in the well-being of children and adolescents, we can create a brighter future for all.

- Teenage Years and Beyond

The teenage years are a critical period of development, characterized by significant physical, cognitive, and socio-emotional changes. Adolescents are transitioning from childhood to adulthood, and this period is marked by increasing independence, exploration, and self-discovery. This stage of life is often described as a time of turmoil and turbulence, as teenagers navigate the challenges of identity formation, peer pressure, and societal expectations. However, it is also a time of immense growth and opportunity, as adolescents begin to shape their identities, establish goals for the future, and develop important social and emotional skills.

One of the key developmental tasks of adolescence is the formation of a coherent and stable sense of self. During this time, teenagers are exploring different roles, values, and beliefs, and are trying to understand who they are and what they want out of life. This process of identity formation is influenced by various factors, including family, peers, school, and media. Adolescents often experiment with different identities and personas as they try to find a sense of belonging and purpose. This can lead to conflicts and confusion, as teenagers struggle to reconcile their inner selves with the external pressures and expectations placed upon them. However, this period of exploration and self-discovery is essential for building a strong sense of self and developing a clear sense of identity.

Peer relationships play a crucial role in the lives of adolescents, as teenagers begin to establish their independence and form connections outside of their family. Peer relationships provide a sense of belonging, support, and validation, and can have a significant impact on adolescent development. Friends serve as sources of social comparison, influence, and encouragement, shaping teenagers' attitudes, behaviors, and self-perceptions. Peer pressure is a common feature of adolescence, as teenagers are often swayed by their friends to conform to group norms and engage in risky behaviors. However, peer relationships can also be a source of empowerment, as friends provide emotional support, companionship, and opportunities for social learning and growth. Positive peer relationships can enhance adolescents' self-esteem, social skills, and resilience, while negative peer relationships can lead to feelings of isolation, rejection, and low self-worth.

Cognitive development during adolescence is marked by significant changes in thinking, reasoning, and decision-making abilities. The teenage brain is undergoing a process of maturation, as neural pathways are pruned and refined, and new connections are formed. This period of brain development is characterized by increased synaptic pruning, myelination, and synaptic plasticity, which contribute to improvements in cognitive functions such as attention, memory, and executive functioning. Adolescents are better able to think abstractly, critically analyze information, and consider multiple perspectives, as their cognitive abilities become more advanced and sophisticated. However, this period of cognitive development is also marked by impulsivity, risk-taking behavior, and emotional reactivity, as the prefrontal cortex, which is responsible for inhibitory control and decision-making, continues to develop throughout adolescence. This can make teenagers more susceptible to peer pressure, sensation-seeking, and engaging in risky behaviors.

Socio-emotional development during adolescence is characterized by significant changes in social relationships, emotions, and self-regulation. Teenagers are experiencing heightened emotional intensity, as they grapple with a wide range of emotions, including joy, sadness, anger, fear, and excitement. Adolescents are also learning to regulate their emotions, manage stress, and cope with challenges, as they develop important social and emotional skills. This period of socio-emotional development is marked by the emergence of self-awareness, empathy, and perspective-taking abilities, as teenagers become more attuned to their own emotions and the feelings of others. Adolescents are also forming close relationships with peers, romantic partners, and mentors, as they navigate the complexities of intimacy, trust, and loyalty. These relationships provide opportunities for emotional intimacy, social support, and personal growth, as teenagers learn to communicate effectively, resolve conflicts, and establish healthy boundaries.

As adolescents navigate the challenges and opportunities of the teenage years, it is important for parents, teachers, and other caring adults to provide guidance, support, and encouragement. Adolescents need adults who can listen to their concerns, validate their experiences, and offer practical advice and assistance. The teenage years can be a confusing and overwhelming time, and teenagers may benefit from the support of trusted adults who can help them navigate the complexities of adolescence. Parents can foster open communication, set clear boundaries, and provide opportunities for independence and autonomy, while also offering guidance, structure, and supervision. Teachers can create positive learning environments, provide opportunities for growth and achievement, and offer emotional support and encouragement. By working together to support and empower adolescents, adults can help teenagers thrive during the teenage years and beyond, as they transition into adulthood and pursue their goals and aspirations.

Chapter 3: Communication Strategies for Parents

- EFFECTIVE LISTENING Skills

Effective listening skills are crucial in various aspects of life, spanning from personal relationships to professional settings. Listening is an essential component of communication, as it enables individuals to understand and respond appropriately to the messages they receive. When people are actively listened to, they feel valued and respected, leading to stronger connections and improved outcomes. In contrast, poor listening can result in misunderstandings, conflict, and missed opportunities for collaboration and growth.

To develop effective listening skills, individuals must cultivate several key qualities, including empathy, patience, and focus. Empathy involves putting oneself in the other person's shoes and trying to understand their perspective and emotions. This allows for a deeper connection and a more meaningful exchange of ideas. Patience is essential in listening, as it requires giving the speaker enough time to express themselves fully without interruptions or premature judgments. Additionally, focus is crucial for effective listening, as it involves dedicating one's full attention to the speaker and being present in the moment.

Active listening is a technique that can significantly enhance one's listening skills. This involves not only hearing the words spoken by the speaker but also paying attention to their tone of voice, body language, and underlying emotions. Active listening requires engaging with the speaker by asking clarifying questions, providing affirmations, and summarizing key points. By actively listening, individuals demonstrate their genuine interest in the speaker and create a supportive and collaborative environment for communication.

One common obstacle to effective listening is the tendency to engage in selective listening, where individuals only pay attention to information that aligns with their preconceived notions or interests. This can lead to misunderstandings and barriers to effective communication. To overcome selective listening, individuals must practice open-mindedness and flexibility in their approach to listening. By being receptive to new ideas and perspectives, individuals can expand their understanding and improve their communication skills.

Cultural differences can also impact listening skills, as individuals from diverse backgrounds may have different norms and expectations regarding communication. It is essential to be mindful of cultural differences in listening styles and adapt one's approach accordingly. By showing respect for cultural diversity and being open to learning from others, individuals can enhance their listening skills and build stronger connections across cultural boundaries. By cultivating qualities such as empathy, patience, and focus, individuals can improve their listening skills and establish meaningful connections with others. Active listening techniques, such as engaging with the speaker and paying attention to verbal and nonverbal cues, can enhance communication and foster collaboration. Overcoming obstacles such as selective listening and cultural differences can further improve listening skills and contribute to more effective communication. Ultimately, by honing their listening skills, individuals can foster stronger relationships, resolve conflicts, and achieve success in their personal and professional lives.

- Encouraging Open and Honest Conversations

Encouraging open and honest conversations is essential for building strong relationships, fostering trust, and promoting effective communication in both personal and professional settings. In today's fast-paced and digital world, it can be easy to avoid difficult conversations or shy away from expressing our true thoughts and feelings. However, by creating a culture that values open and honest communication, we can create a supportive environment where people feel comfortable sharing their ideas, feedback, and concerns.

One of the first steps in encouraging open and honest conversations is to create a safe space where individuals feel comfortable speaking their minds without fear of judgement or reprisal. This can be achieved by setting clear expectations for communication, fostering a culture of respect and empathy, and actively listening to others' perspectives. It is important to create an atmosphere where everyone feels valued and heard, regardless of their position or background. By creating a sense of psychological safety, individuals will be more likely to share their thoughts and feelings openly.

Another key aspect of encouraging open and honest conversations is to lead by example. As a leader or facilitator, it is important to model transparent communication and encourage others to do the same. This can involve sharing your own thoughts and feelings, being open to feedback, and demonstrating active listening skills. By showing vulnerability and authenticity, you can create a sense of trust and openness that will encourage others to do the same.

In addition to modeling open communication, it is important to provide training and support to help individuals develop the skills and confidence needed to engage in honest conversations. This can include providing resources on effective communication techniques, conflict resolution strategies, and active listening skills. By investing in communication training, organizations can empower their employees to navigate difficult conversations with confidence and professionalism.

Furthermore, it is important to create opportunities for open and honest conversations to occur naturally within the organization. This can involve regular team meetings, feedback sessions, one-on-one discussions, and team-building activities. By creating a culture that values open communication, organizations can foster a sense of collaboration, innovation, and trust among employees. Encouraging open and honest conversations can lead to greater transparency, improved problem-solving, and stronger relationships within the organization. By creating a safe space, leading by example, providing training and support, and creating opportunities for dialogue, organizations can empower their employees to engage in honest conversations with confidence and professionalism. By valuing open communication, organizations can create a culture of trust, collaboration, and innovation that will benefit both the individuals and the organization as a whole.

- Navigating Difficult Topics

Navigating difficult topics is a crucial skill in both professional and personal settings. Whether it be discussing challenging issues in the workplace or having sensitive conversations with friends and family, being able to navigate these topics with grace and sensitivity is essential for effective communication and relationship-building. Difficult topics can range from disagreements over work assignments to discussing more complex and sensitive topics such as race, politics, or personal values. While these conversations may be uncomfortable or intimidating, they are necessary for fostering understanding, building trust, and resolving conflicts.

One key aspect of navigating difficult topics is to approach the conversation with an open mind and a willingness to listen. It is important to practice active listening and to truly hear and understand the perspectives of others, even if they differ from your own. This can help to foster empathy and create a sense of mutual respect, even when discussing challenging or contentious topics. By approaching the conversation with an open mind, you can create a safe space for honest and respectful dialogue, which is essential for finding common ground and reaching a resolution.

Another important aspect of navigating difficult topics is to choose the right time and place for the conversation. It is important to ensure that both parties are in a calm and receptive state of mind before engaging in a difficult conversation. This may involve scheduling a specific time to talk, finding a private and comfortable setting, or ensuring that there are no distractions or interruptions. By creating a conducive environment for the conversation, you can help to minimize conflict and create a more productive and positive dialogue.

Furthermore, it is important to set clear goals and objectives for the conversation and to establish ground rules for communication. This may include agreeing to speak respectfully, avoiding personal attacks or accusations, and focusing on finding solutions or compromises rather than dwelling on past grievances. By setting clear expectations and boundaries for the conversation, you can create a constructive and productive dialogue that can lead to resolution and understanding.

In addition, it is important to practice empathy and emotional intelligence when navigating difficult topics. This involves being aware of your own emotions and reactions, as well as being able to understand and respond to the emotions of others. By demonstrating empathy and understanding, you can create a sense of trust and rapport that can help to facilitate a more open and honest conversation. Being able to recognize and validate the emotions of others, even if you do not agree with their perspective, can help to create a sense of mutual respect and understanding.

Moreover, it is important to approach difficult topics with a growth mindset and a willingness to learn and grow from the conversation. Rather than seeing conflicts or disagreements as threats, view them as opportunities for personal and professional growth. By being open to feedback and willing to reflect on your own beliefs and assumptions, you can create a more inclusive and understanding environment that promotes meaningful dialogue and mutual respect. Embracing diversity of thought and perspective can help to foster innovation, creativity, and collaboration in both personal and professional settings. By approaching these conversations with an open mind, choosing the right time and place, setting clear goals and ground rules, practicing empathy and emotional intelligence, and embracing a growth mindset, you can create a more productive and positive dialogue that fosters understanding and resolution. By navigating difficult topics with grace and sensitivity, you can build stronger relationships, foster trust and respect, and create a more inclusive and collaborative environment that promotes personal and professional growth.

Chapter 4: Understanding Your Daughter's Emotions

- EXPLORING THE EMOTIONAL Landscape of Girls

Adolescence is a time of immense change and development, both physically and emotionally. For girls in particular, this period can be especially tumultuous as they navigate the complexities of identity formation and social pressures. As they grapple with societal expectations and norms, girls often find themselves in a emotional landscape that can be both exhilarating and challenging.

One key aspect of the emotional landscape of girls is the pressure to conform to gender stereotypes and expectations. From a young age, girls are bombarded with messages about how they should look, act, and behave. This pressure to fit into a certain mold can have a profound impact on their self-esteem and sense of worth. Many girls internalize these messages, leading to feelings of inadequacy and self-doubt. As they strive to meet these external expectations, girls may struggle to express their true emotions and desires, leading to a sense of disconnection from their authentic selves.

Another important aspect of the emotional landscape of girls is the role of relationships in shaping their emotions. During adolescence, girls often place a strong emphasis on their relationships with peers and romantic partners. These relationships can be a source of immense joy and fulfillment, but they can also be a source of conflict and heartache. As girls navigate the highs and lows of friendship and romantic entanglements, they may experience a wide range of emotions, from elation and love to jealousy and betrayal. These emotional experiences can have a lasting impact on their sense of self and their ability to form healthy, fulfilling relationships in the future.

One of the most crucial aspects of the emotional landscape of girls is the pressure to conform to societal expectations while also asserting their own agency and autonomy. Girls are often expected to be polite, nurturing, and accommodating, while also being assertive, ambitious, and independent. This conflicting set of expectations can create a sense of internal conflict and confusion, as girls grapple with the tension between who they are expected to be and who they truly are. This struggle to balance societal expectations with personal desires can create a deep sense of emotional turmoil and uncertainty, as girls try to navigate the complexities of their evolving identity. By acknowledging and addressing these complexities, we can better support girls as they navigate the challenges of adolescence and develop into confident, resilient young women. It is essential that we create a supportive and empowering environment for girls to explore and express their emotions, so that they can develop a strong sense of self and navigate the complexities of the emotional landscape with confidence and resilience.

- Helping Your Daughter Manage Stress and Anxiety

Adolescence is a time of significant change and growth for young girls. As they navigate the challenges of school, social relationships, and personal development, it is not uncommon for them to experience stress and anxiety. It is important for parents to be aware of the signs of stress and anxiety in their daughters and to provide them with the support and tools they need to manage these feelings effectively.

One of the first steps in helping your daughter manage stress and anxiety is to create an open and supportive environment where she feels comfortable discussing her feelings. Encourage your daughter to talk to you about what is causing her stress and anxiety and listen without judgment. Let her know that it is normal to experience these feelings and that you are there to support her through them. By creating a safe space for your daughter to express her emotions, you can help her feel understood and validated, which can be a powerful tool in managing stress and anxiety.

In addition to providing emotional support, there are practical steps you can take to help your daughter manage stress and anxiety. Encourage her to engage in regular physical activity, such as exercise or sports, which can help reduce stress and improve mood. Encourage her to prioritize self-care activities, such as getting enough sleep, eating a healthy diet, and taking time to relax and unwind. By taking care of her physical and emotional well-being, your daughter can build resilience and better cope with the challenges she faces.

Another important way to help your daughter manage stress and anxiety is to teach her effective coping strategies. Encourage her to practice mindfulness and relaxation techniques, such as deep breathing exercises or meditation, which can help calm the mind and body in times of stress. Teach her to challenge negative thought patterns and reframe stressful situations in a more positive light. Encourage her to seek support from friends, teachers, or counselors if she is struggling to cope with stress and anxiety on her own.

It is also important to help your daughter set realistic goals and manage her time effectively. Encourage her to break large tasks into smaller, more manageable steps, and to prioritize her time and energy on the most important tasks. Help her develop good study habits and organizational skills to reduce feelings of overwhelm and improve her academic performance. By helping your daughter set achievable goals and manage her time effectively, you can empower her to take control of her stress and anxiety and build her confidence in her abilities.

To bring to a close, it is important to be aware of when your daughter may need professional help to manage her stress and anxiety. If her symptoms persist or interfere with her daily life, it may be necessary to seek guidance from a mental health professional. A therapist or counselor can help your daughter develop coping strategies, manage her emotions, and build resilience to better navigate the challenges of adolescence. By seeking professional help when needed, you can ensure that your daughter receives the support and care she needs to thrive and succeed. By creating a supportive environment, teaching effective coping strategies, and encouraging healthy habits, you can empower your daughter to build resilience and navigate the challenges of adolescence with confidence and strength. Remember to be patient and understanding as your daughter learns to manage stress and anxiety, and always prioritize her well-being and mental health above all else. With your love and support, your daughter can overcome stress and anxiety and emerge stronger and more resilient on the other side.

- Teaching Emotional Regulation and Resilience

Emotional regulation and resilience are essential skills that play a pivotal role in an individual's overall well-being and success in various aspects of life. Teaching these skills is crucial in helping individuals effectively manage their emotions, navigate challenging situations, and bounce back from adversity. Emotional regulation refers to the ability to understand, manage, and respond to emotional experiences in a healthy and productive manner. It involves being able to recognize and label one's emotions, regulate their intensity, and express them in appropriate ways.

Teaching emotional regulation can have a profound impact on individuals' mental health and interpersonal relationships. By learning how to regulate their emotions, individuals can reduce stress, anxiety, and other negative emotions, leading to improved overall well-being. Additionally, emotional regulation skills can help individuals communicate more effectively, resolve conflicts, and build stronger connections with others. By teaching emotional regulation, educators can empower individuals to navigate and cope with the complex emotions that arise in everyday life.

Resilience, on the other hand, refers to the ability to bounce back from adversity, overcome challenges, and adapt to change. It is a key component of mental and emotional well-being and plays a critical role in determining how individuals respond to setbacks and difficulties. Teaching resilience involves helping individuals develop the skills and qualities needed to navigate challenging situations and emerge stronger from them. This includes fostering a positive attitude, building problem-solving skills, and fostering a sense of self-efficacy and control.

Educators can play a crucial role in teaching emotional regulation and resilience by creating a supportive and nurturing learning environment that promotes these skills. By incorporating social-emotional learning into the curriculum, educators can provide students with the tools and strategies they need to regulate their emotions and build resilience. This can involve teaching students how to identify and express their emotions, develop coping mechanisms, and practice self-care. Educators can also teach students how to set goals, persevere in the face of challenges, and bounce back from setbacks.

In addition to incorporating social-emotional learning into the curriculum, educators can also use various teaching strategies and techniques to help students develop emotional regulation and resilience. This can include modeling healthy emotional regulation behaviors, providing opportunities for students to practice coping skills, and offering emotional support and encouragement. Educators can also create a safe and inclusive learning environment where students feel comfortable expressing their emotions and seeking support when needed.

Teaching emotional regulation and resilience is not only beneficial for students' mental health and well-being but also for their academic success. Research has shown that students who have strong emotional regulation and resilience skills are more likely to have better academic performance, attendance, and behavior. By teaching these skills, educators can help students thrive in the classroom and beyond, setting them up for success in their personal and professional lives. By providing students with the tools and strategies they need to regulate their emotions and build resilience, educators can empower them to navigate challenges, overcome setbacks, and thrive in an ever-changing world. By incorporating social-emotional learning into the curriculum and using effective teaching strategies, educators can help students develop the skills they need to become resilient, emotionally intelligent, and successful individuals.

Chapter 5: Building Self-Esteem and Confidence

- RECOGNIZING AND CELEBRATING Your Daughter's Strengths

Recognizing and celebrating your daughter's strengths is an essential aspect of fostering her overall development and self-esteem. As parents, it is our responsibility to provide a supportive and nurturing environment where our daughters can thrive and feel empowered to reach their full potential. By acknowledging and celebrating their strengths, we are helping them build confidence and resilience that will serve them well in various aspects of life.

One of the first steps in recognizing your daughter's strengths is to observe her closely and pay attention to her unique talents, abilities, and interests. This may involve spending quality time with her, engaging in meaningful conversations, and actively listening to her thoughts and feelings. By being attuned to her inner world, you can gain valuable insights into what makes her tick and what brings her joy. This awareness will help you identify areas where she excels and where she may need additional support or encouragement.

It is also important to provide your daughter with opportunities to explore and develop her strengths. This may involve enrolling her in activities or programs that align with her interests, such as music lessons, sports teams, or art classes. By encouraging her to pursue her passions and hone her skills, you are helping her build confidence and a sense of accomplishment. It is also important to offer praise and positive reinforcement when she demonstrates her strengths, as this will reinforce her self-belief and motivation to continue growing and expanding her abilities.

In addition to recognizing and celebrating your daughter's individual strengths, it is also important to cultivate a positive and empowering mindset in your family dynamic. This can involve fostering a culture of respect, support, and encouragement where all family members are valued for their unique qualities and contributions. By creating a safe and nurturing environment where your daughter feels accepted and celebrated for who she is, you are instilling in her a sense of self-worth and confidence that will carry over into other areas of her life.

Furthermore, it is important to model and encourage a growth mindset in your daughter, where she sees challenges and setbacks as opportunities for growth and learning. By teaching her to embrace resilience and perseverance in the face of adversity, you are equipping her with the tools she needs to navigate the ups and downs of life with grace and confidence. By fostering a growth mindset in your daughter, you are helping her build resilience, tenacity, and a sense of agency that will serve her well in her personal and professional pursuits.

Ultimately, recognizing and celebrating your daughter's strengths is a powerful way to help her build confidence, resilience, and a sense of self-worth. By acknowledging and nurturing her unique talents and abilities, you are empowering her to reach her full potential and thrive in all aspects of her life. As parents, it is our privilege and responsibility to provide our daughters with the support, encouragement, and guidance they need to flourish and succeed. By fostering a positive and empowering environment where your daughter's strengths are recognized and celebrated, you are laying the foundation for her to become a confident, resilient, and empowered individual who can overcome any challenge life may throw her way.

- Empowering Your Daughter to Embrace Her Potential

Empowering your daughter to embrace her potential is a crucial aspect of parenting and personal development. As a parent, it is important to instill confidence, self-worth, and a sense of purpose in your daughter from a young age. By providing her with the necessary tools and encouragement, you can help her unlock her full potential and achieve her goals and dreams.

One of the first steps in empowering your daughter is to ensure that she has a strong sense of self-esteem. This can be achieved by praising her efforts and accomplishments, no matter how small they may seem. Additionally, it is important to teach her to value herself and her unique qualities, rather than comparing herself to others. By instilling a sense of self-worth in your daughter, you can help her develop the confidence needed to pursue her passions and achieve success.

In addition to building self-esteem, it is important to encourage your daughter to explore her interests and talents. By exposing her to a variety of activities and experiences, you can help her discover her passions and talents. Whether it is through sports, music, art, or academics, it is important to support and encourage your daughter to pursue her interests and dreams. By providing her with opportunities to excel in areas that she is passionate about, you can help her develop a sense of purpose and fulfillment.

Furthermore, it is important to teach your daughter the value of resilience and perseverance. Life is full of challenges and setbacks, and it is important for your daughter to learn how to overcome obstacles and bounce back from failures. By teaching her to view setbacks as opportunities for growth and learning, you can help her develop the resilience needed to navigate life's ups and downs. Encouraging your daughter to persevere in the face of challenges will help her develop the grit and determination needed to achieve her goals and dreams.

Another important aspect of empowering your daughter is to provide her with the skills and knowledge needed to navigate the world around her. This includes teaching her about financial literacy, communication skills, and goal setting. By equipping your daughter with the tools she needs to succeed, you can help her build a solid foundation for a successful future. Additionally, it is important to encourage your daughter to take risks and step outside of her comfort zone. By pushing her boundaries and trying new things, you can help her develop the confidence and resilience needed to embrace her potential.

In closing, it is important to be a positive role model for your daughter. Children learn by example, and as a parent, it is important to demonstrate the values and behaviors that you want to instill in your daughter. By showing her what it means to be confident, resilient, and determined, you can inspire her to embrace her potential and pursue her dreams. Additionally, it is important to provide a supportive and nurturing environment for your daughter to thrive in. By creating a safe and loving space for her to grow and learn, you can help her develop the self-esteem and confidence needed to reach her full potential. By providing her with the necessary tools, encouragement, and support, you can help your daughter unlock her full potential and achieve her goals and dreams. Remember to instill confidence, self-worth, and a sense of purpose in your daughter, while also teaching her the value of resilience, perseverance, and self-discovery. By being a positive role model and creating a supportive environment for her to thrive in, you can help your daughter develop the skills and mindset needed to navigate life's challenges and reach her full potential.

- Overcoming Common Confidence Challenges

Confidence is an essential trait that can greatly impact a person's success in both professional and personal endeavors. However, many individuals struggle with confidence challenges that can hinder their ability to reach their full potential. In this article, we will explore some common confidence challenges that people face and provide practical strategies for overcoming them.

One of the most common confidence challenges is self-doubt. Many people struggle with questioning their abilities and second-guessing themselves, which can greatly undermine their confidence. This self-doubt often stems from fear of failure or the belief that one is not capable of achieving their goals. To overcome self-doubt, it is important to challenge negative thought patterns and replace them with more positive and empowering beliefs. This can be done through affirmations, visualization techniques, and seeking support from friends, family, or a therapist.

Another common confidence challenge is imposter syndrome. Imposter syndrome is the feeling that one does not deserve their successes and that they will be exposed as a fraud. This can be particularly prevalent among high-achieving individuals who constantly feel the need to prove themselves. To overcome imposter syndrome, it is important to acknowledge and celebrate one's accomplishments, focus on personal growth rather than comparison to others, and seek feedback and validation from trusted sources.

Perfectionism is another confidence challenge that many people struggle with. Perfectionists often set impossibly high standards for themselves and are overly critical of their own performance. This can lead to a fear of failure and a reluctance to take risks. To overcome perfectionism, it is important to embrace imperfection and see failures as opportunities for growth. Setting realistic goals and learning to be kinder to oneself can help to build confidence and resilience.

Social anxiety is a common confidence challenge that can make it difficult for individuals to assert themselves in social situations. People with social anxiety may feel self-conscious, nervous, or awkward in social settings, which can hold them back from forming meaningful connections or pursuing their goals. To overcome social anxiety, it is important to practice social skills, challenge negative thoughts about oneself, and gradually expose oneself to social situations in a safe and supportive environment.

To bring to a close, fear of rejection is a common confidence challenge that can prevent individuals from taking risks and putting themselves out there. The fear of being judged or criticized by others can be paralyzing and can lead to missed opportunities for growth and success. To overcome the fear of rejection, it is important to reframe rejection as a natural part of life that does not define one's worth. Building resilience and self-compassion can help individuals to bounce back from rejection and continue to pursue their goals with confidence. By identifying and addressing these challenges, individuals can build the self-confidence and resilience needed to overcome setbacks and achieve their full potential. By practicing self-care, challenging negative thought patterns, seeking support from others, and taking risks, individuals can overcome common confidence challenges and thrive in all areas of their lives.

Chapter 6: Nurturing Mental Health and Well-being

- IDENTIFYING SIGNS of Mental Health Concerns

Mental health is an essential component of overall well-being, yet it is often overlooked or misunderstood. Many individuals may be experiencing mental health concerns without even realizing it, which can have serious repercussions on their daily functioning and quality of life. It is crucial for everyone to be able to recognize signs of mental health concerns in themselves and others, in order to seek appropriate support and treatment.

One of the most common signs of mental health concerns is a persistent change in mood or behavior. This can manifest as prolonged feelings of sadness, anxiety, or irritability, as well as sudden and unexplained shifts in mood. Individuals may also isolate themselves from friends and family, lose interest in activities they once enjoyed, or experience changes in sleep patterns and appetite. These changes can be subtle and gradual, making them easy to dismiss or ignore. However, paying attention to these shifts and seeking help early on can prevent further deterioration of mental health.

Another important sign of mental health concerns is difficulty concentrating or making decisions. Individuals may find it challenging to focus on tasks, remember important information, or complete daily responsibilities. This can lead to poor performance at work or school, as well as strained relationships with others. Furthermore, individuals may experience racing thoughts, confusion, or indecisiveness, which can significantly impact their ability to function effectively in various aspects of their lives. Recognizing these cognitive symptoms can help individuals seek appropriate interventions and support to improve their mental well-being.

Physical symptoms can also indicate underlying mental health concerns. It is not uncommon for individuals to experience physical ailments such as headaches, stomachaches, or muscle tension in response to stress or emotional distress. These symptoms may not have a clear physical cause and may persist despite medical treatment. Additionally, individuals may engage in harmful behaviors such as substance abuse, self-harm, or reckless driving as a means of coping with their mental health issues. These behaviors can further exacerbate their mental health concerns and put them at risk for serious consequences. Recognizing the connection between physical symptoms and mental health is crucial for individuals to address their underlying issues effectively.

Social and interpersonal difficulties can also signal mental health concerns. Individuals may struggle to maintain relationships with others, exhibit distrust or paranoia, or engage in conflict with loved ones. These interpersonal challenges can stem from underlying mental health issues such as depression, anxiety, or trauma. Individuals may also experience difficulties with communication, assertiveness, or boundaries, which can lead to strained relationships and isolation. Recognizing these social symptoms can help individuals seek therapy, support groups, or other interventions to improve their relationships and overall mental well-being. By recognizing changes in mood, behavior, cognition, physical health, and social interactions, individuals can take proactive steps to improve their mental well-being and quality of life. It is important to approach these signs with compassion, understanding, and a willingness to seek help from professionals when needed. Remember, mental health concerns are common and treatable, and seeking support is a sign of strength, not weakness. Let us work together to promote awareness of mental health issues and support one another in our journeys toward healing and wellness.

- Seeking Professional Help When Needed

Seeking professional help when needed is a crucial step in maintaining mental health and overall well-being. It is important to recognize that we all face challenges and struggles at some point in our lives, and it is completely normal to seek help from a trained professional when those challenges become overwhelming. Whether you are dealing with feelings of anxiety, depression, stress, or any other mental health issue, reaching out to a therapist, counselor, psychologist, or psychiatrist can provide the support and guidance you need to navigate through those difficulties.

There is often a stigma attached to seeking professional help for mental health issues, but it is important to remember that seeking help is a sign of strength, not weakness. It takes courage to acknowledge that you may need assistance and to take steps to improve your mental health. Professional therapists and counselors are trained to provide a safe and non-judgmental space for individuals to explore their thoughts and feelings, and to develop coping strategies to better manage their mental health concerns.

It is also important to recognize that mental health professionals have the expertise and training to provide tailored treatment plans that are personalized to meet your specific needs. They can offer evidence-based therapies, such as cognitive-behavioral therapy, dialectical behavior therapy, and mindfulness-based therapies, that have been proven to be effective in treating a wide range of mental health issues. By working with a mental health professional, you can develop the skills and strategies to better cope with the challenges you are facing and to improve your overall quality of life.

In addition to individual therapy, mental health professionals can also provide valuable support through group therapy, family therapy, and couples therapy. These therapeutic approaches can help you improve your communication skills, deepen your relationships, and develop healthy coping mechanisms in a supportive and collaborative environment. By engaging in therapy with your loved ones, you can work together to address any underlying issues and strengthen your connections with one another.

When considering seeking professional help, it is important to find a mental health professional who is a good fit for you. This may involve researching different therapists or counselors in your area, asking for recommendations from friends or family members, or seeking referrals from your primary care provider. It is also important to consider factors such as the therapist's approach and treatment methods, their experience working with individuals who have similar concerns to yours, and their availability for appointments.

It is also important to communicate openly and honestly with your mental health professional about your concerns, goals, and expectations for therapy. This can help ensure that you are both on the same page and working towards the same objectives. Your therapist or counselor is there to support you and guide you through the therapeutic process, so it is important to be an active participant in your own treatment and to be willing to engage in the work that is necessary for your mental health to improve. It is important to remember that it is okay to ask for help and that there is no shame in reaching out to a therapist, counselor, psychologist, or psychiatrist when you are struggling. By working with a mental health professional, you can develop the skills and strategies to better cope with life's challenges, improve your relationships, and enhance your quality of life. Remember, you are not alone in your struggles, and help is available to support you on your journey towards mental wellness.

- Creating a Supportive Environment for Your Daughter's Emotional Health

Creating a supportive environment for your daughter's emotional health is essential for her overall well-being and development. As parents, it is important to prioritize your daughter's emotional needs and provide her with the necessary tools and resources to navigate through life's challenges. By fostering a safe and nurturing environment, you can help your daughter build resilience, develop healthy coping mechanisms, and cultivate positive relationships.

One of the first steps in creating a supportive environment for your daughter's emotional health is open communication. Encourage your daughter to express her feelings and emotions freely, without fear of judgment or criticism. Listen actively and empathetically when she shares her thoughts, and validate her experiences. By creating a safe space for her to communicate, you can help her build confidence in expressing her emotions and seeking support when needed.

In addition to open communication, it is important to model healthy coping mechanisms for your daughter. Show her how to manage stress, handle difficult situations, and practice self-care. By demonstrating positive behaviors and coping strategies, you can help your daughter learn how to navigate through challenging emotions and build resilience. Encourage her to engage in activities that promote relaxation and self-care, such as exercise, mindfulness, and creative outlets.

Furthermore, fostering a supportive environment for your daughter's emotional health involves building strong and positive relationships. Encourage your daughter to form connections with friends, family members, and mentors who provide support, encouragement, and guidance. Help her develop social skills, empathy, and emotional intelligence, so she can navigate through interpersonal relationships effectively. By nurturing her relationships, you can help your daughter feel connected, valued, and loved.

Creating a supportive environment for your daughter's emotional health also involves setting boundaries and establishing routines. Provide structure and consistency in her daily life, so she knows what to expect and feels a sense of security. Set clear expectations, rules, and limits that promote safety, respect, and responsibility. By creating a predictable and stable environment, you can help your daughter feel grounded and empowered to navigate through life's challenges.

Moreover, it is important to educate yourself about mental health and emotional well-being, so you can better support your daughter. Stay informed about the signs and symptoms of common mental health issues, such as anxiety, depression, and stress. Seek professional guidance and resources if needed, and encourage your daughter to access mental health support when necessary. By being proactive and knowledgeable about mental health, you can help your daughter build a strong foundation for emotional well-being. By prioritizing her emotional needs, fostering open communication, modeling healthy coping mechanisms, building positive relationships, setting boundaries, and educating yourself about mental health, you can help your daughter develop resilience, self-awareness, and emotional intelligence. Ultimately, by providing a safe and nurturing environment for your daughter, you can empower her to navigate through life's challenges with confidence and grace.

Chapter 7: Navigating Peer Relationships

- UNDERSTANDING THE Dynamics of Friendship

Friendship is a fundamental aspect of human life that plays a crucial role in our emotional well-being and overall happiness. It is a unique and complex relationship that involves mutual trust, support, and affection between individuals. While friendships can differ in many ways, they all share common dynamics that contribute to the strength and longevity of the bond. Understanding these dynamics can help us cultivate and maintain healthy and fulfilling friendships throughout our lives.

One of the key dynamics of friendship is reciprocity, which refers to the mutual give-and-take that characterizes the relationship. This means that both friends contribute to the friendship in equal measure, whether it be through emotional support, companionship, or shared experiences. Reciprocity is essential for maintaining balance and harmony in the friendship, as it ensures that both parties feel valued and appreciated. When there is an imbalance in reciprocity, with one friend always giving more than they receive, it can lead to feelings of resentment and insecurity, ultimately weakening the bond.

Another important dynamic of friendship is trust, which is the foundation of any healthy relationship. Trust involves having confidence in your friend's honesty, reliability, and loyalty, and believing that they have your best interests at heart. Trust is built over time through consistent and honest communication, reliability, and mutual respect. When trust is broken, whether through betrayal or dishonesty, it can be difficult to repair the friendship and may lead to long-lasting damage. Therefore, it is essential to foster trust in your friendships by being transparent, reliable, and respectful towards your friends.

Communication is also a vital dynamic of friendship, as it is the primary way in which friends connect, express their thoughts and feelings, and resolve conflicts. Effective communication involves active listening, empathy, and open and honest expression of emotions. It is important to communicate openly with your friends and encourage them to do the same, as this can help strengthen your bond and prevent misunderstandings or conflicts from escalating. By being a good listener, offering support, and expressing your thoughts and feelings clearly, you can foster a sense of intimacy and understanding in your friendships.

Mutual respect is another key dynamic of friendship, as it involves recognizing and valuing each other's differences, opinions, and boundaries. Respect is essential for maintaining a healthy and harmonious relationship, as it lays the foundation for trust, communication, and mutual support. By respecting your friend's values, beliefs, and boundaries, you can create a safe and inclusive space where both of you feel comfortable expressing yourselves and being authentic. It is important to treat your friends with kindness, consideration, and empathy, and to avoid judgment or criticism, as this can erode trust and damage the friendship.

Empathy is also a crucial dynamic of friendship, as it involves the ability to understand and share your friend's emotions, perspectives, and experiences. Empathy allows you to connect on a deeper level with your friend, to provide support and comfort during difficult times, and to celebrate their successes and joys. By showing empathy towards your friends, you can strengthen your bond and create a sense of mutual understanding and connection. It is important to listen attentively to your friend's feelings, validate their experiences, and offer support and encouragement when needed. Empathy can help bridge the gap between differences in opinion or perspective and foster compassion and understanding in your friendships.

Lastly, shared experiences and memories are important dynamics of friendship, as they create a sense of history, camaraderie, and connection between friends. Whether it be fun adventures, challenging situations, or significant milestones, shared experiences help strengthen the bond between friends and nurture a sense of belonging and togetherness. By creating and cherishing memories together, you can build a strong foundation for your friendship and create a sense of shared identity that strengthens your bond over time. It is important to actively engage in activities and share moments with your friends to create lasting memories and deepen your connection. By understanding and embracing these dynamics, you can cultivate and maintain healthy and fulfilling friendships that contribute to your emotional well-being and overall happiness. Remember to nurture your friendships through reciprocity, trust, communication, respect, empathy, and shared experiences, and to cherish and celebrate the unique connection you share with your friends. Friendship is a precious gift that enriches our lives and brings joy and meaning to our existence, so invest in your friendships and cultivate them with love, care, and appreciation.

- Addressing Social Pressures and Bullying

Addressing social pressures and bullying is a crucial issue that affects individuals of all ages and backgrounds. Social pressures can come in many forms, from peer pressure to conform to certain behaviors or beliefs, to societal expectations that dictate how we should look, act, or think. This can create a hostile environment where individuals feel the need to conform in order to fit in or avoid being ostracized. Bullying, on the other hand, involves one person or group exerting power and control over another through intimidation, harassment, or violence. This can have a devastating impact on the victim's mental and emotional well-being, as well as their physical safety.

One of the key ways to address social pressures and bullying is through education and awareness. By raising awareness about the prevalence and harmful effects of social pressures and bullying, we can empower individuals to recognize and address these issues. Schools, communities, and workplaces play a crucial role in educating people about the impact of social pressures and bullying, and providing them with the tools and resources to stand up against these behaviors. This can include promoting empathy, tolerance, and respect for diversity, as well as teaching conflict resolution skills and promoting positive social interactions.

Another important aspect of addressing social pressures and bullying is creating a supportive and inclusive environment where individuals feel safe and accepted for who they are. This involves fostering a culture of respect and kindness, where differences are celebrated rather than ridiculed. This can be achieved through promoting diversity and inclusion initiatives, establishing anti-bullying policies, and providing resources and support for those who have experienced bullying. By creating a sense of community and belonging, we can help individuals feel empowered to speak out against social pressures and bullying, and seek help when needed.

In addition to education and creating a supportive environment, it is essential to address the root causes of social pressures and bullying. These can include factors such as societal norms and expectations, discrimination and prejudice, and power imbalances. By challenging these structural barriers and promoting equality and justice, we can create a more just and equitable society where everyone can thrive. This can involve advocating for policy changes, promoting social justice initiatives, and empowering marginalized communities to speak up and demand change.

It is also important to address the mental health implications of social pressures and bullying. The impact of these experiences can be profound, leading to feelings of low self-esteem, anxiety, depression, and even suicidal thoughts. It is crucial to provide individuals who have experienced social pressures and bullying with access to mental health support and resources. This can include counseling, therapy, support groups, and crisis intervention services. By addressing the mental health needs of individuals who have experienced bullying, we can help them heal from their trauma and build resilience against future instances of social pressures and bullying. By working together to address these issues, we can create a more inclusive and equitable society where everyone can thrive and feel safe. It is important for individuals, communities, and institutions to take a stand against social pressures and bullying, and to work towards creating a culture of respect, kindness, and acceptance for all. Together, we can make a difference and build a more just and compassionate world for future generations.

- Supporting Healthy Relationships with Peers

Healthy relationships with peers are an essential aspect of personal and social well-being. These relationships provide important sources of emotional support, companionship, and a sense of belonging. They also play a crucial role in shaping our self-esteem, self-confidence, and overall mental health. However, maintaining healthy relationships with peers can sometimes be challenging, especially in today's fast-paced, digital world where communication often takes place through screens rather than face-to-face interactions.

One key factor in supporting healthy relationships with peers is effective communication. Communication is the foundation of any relationship, whether it be with a friend, coworker, or romantic partner. It is important to express your thoughts, feelings, and opinions openly and honestly, while also listening attentively to what others have to say. Active listening is an essential skill that involves giving the speaker your full attention, engaging with their words, and responding appropriately. By communicating effectively and actively listening to our peers, we can build trust, mutual respect, and empathy in our relationships.

Another important aspect of supporting healthy relationships with peers is setting boundaries and respecting the boundaries of others. Boundaries are limits that define what is acceptable and unacceptable behavior in a relationship. By setting clear boundaries, we can protect ourselves from harm, maintain our sense of self-worth, and foster healthy interactions with our peers. It is important to communicate our boundaries openly and assertively, while also respecting the boundaries of others. Having a mutual understanding of each other's boundaries can prevent misunderstandings, conflicts, and hurt feelings in our relationships.

Maintaining a healthy balance between giving and receiving is also crucial in supporting healthy relationships with peers. In any relationship, there should be a fair exchange of support, empathy, and understanding between both parties. It is important to offer assistance and kindness to our peers when they are in need, while also being willing to accept help and care from them in return. By being there for each other in times of joy and sorrow, we can strengthen our bonds with our peers and create a sense of reciprocity and mutual appreciation in our relationships.

Building trust and reliability is another key component of supporting healthy relationships with peers. Trust is the foundation of any successful relationship and is built through consistent and reliable behavior over time. By being honest, dependable, and true to our word, we can earn the trust and confidence of our peers. It is important to follow through on our commitments, be there for our peers when they need us, and be open and transparent in our communication. By demonstrating trustworthiness and reliability in our interactions with others, we can foster a sense of security, safety, and comfort in our relationships.

Lastly, it is important to practice empathy and understanding in our relationships with peers. Empathy is the ability to understand and share the feelings and perspectives of others, and is essential for building strong emotional connections with our peers. By putting ourselves in the shoes of our peers, acknowledging their emotions, and offering support and validation, we can show that we care about their well-being and are willing to listen and help. It is important to be empathetic, compassionate, and non-judgmental in our interactions with others, as this can create a sense of trust, intimacy, and mutual respect in our relationships. By following these principles and cultivating positive qualities in our relationships, we can foster meaningful connections, boost our well-being, and create a supportive and fulfilling social network. Healthy relationships with peers are a valuable asset in our lives and can bring joy, resilience, and a sense of belonging to our personal and social experiences.

Chapter 8: Role Models and Media Influence

- DISCUSSING MEDIA MESSAGES with Your Daughter

In today's fast-paced and technology-driven world, it is more important than ever to have open and honest discussions with our children about the media messages they are exposed to. As parents, we play a crucial role in guiding our children through the often confusing and overwhelming world of media, helping them to decipher the messages they receive and make informed choices about what they consume. This is especially important for young girls, who are often bombarded with harmful and unrealistic messages about beauty, body image, and gender roles.

When discussing media messages with your daughter, it is important to approach the topic with empathy and understanding. Remember that she is constantly being bombarded with messages from a variety of sources, including social media, television, movies, and advertisements. These messages can shape her beliefs and perceptions of herself and the world around her, so it is essential to have open and honest conversations about what she is seeing and how it is affecting her.

One of the most important things you can do when discussing media messages with your daughter is to listen to her thoughts and feelings without judgment. Ask her what she thinks about the media she consumes, and encourage her to express her opinions openly and honestly. By creating a safe and non-judgmental space for your daughter to share her thoughts, you can help her develop critical thinking skills and the ability to analyze and evaluate the messages she receives.

It is also important to help your daughter develop media literacy skills, so she can better understand and interpret the messages she is exposed to. Encourage her to think critically about the media she consumes, asking questions like "who is behind this message. " and "what are they trying to achieve. " By teaching her to question and analyze media messages, you can help her develop a healthy skepticism and a more discerning eye for the media she consumes.

In addition to developing media literacy skills, it is important to help your daughter build a strong sense of self-esteem and body confidence. Media messages often present unrealistic and harmful ideals of beauty and femininity, which can have a negative impact on girls' self-esteem and body image. Encourage your daughter to focus on her strengths and talents, rather than on her appearance, and help her develop a positive body image by emphasizing the importance of health and self-care.

To recapitulate, it is important to set a positive example for your daughter by being mindful of the media messages you consume and how they may influence your own beliefs and behaviors. By being conscious of the media you consume and the messages you endorse, you can show your daughter the importance of critical thinking and self-awareness in navigating the media landscape. Remember that you are your daughter's most important role model, so lead by example and demonstrate healthy media consumption habits in your own life. By approaching the topic with empathy, encouraging open and honest communication, and teaching her to think critically about the media she consumes, you can empower your daughter to make informed choices and cultivate a positive relationship with media. Remember that you are your daughter's most important influence, so lead by example and demonstrate the importance of media literacy and self-awareness in navigating the media landscape. By working together to navigate the media landscape, you can help your daughter develop the skills and confidence she needs to thrive in a media-saturated world.

- Empowering Your Daughter to Think Critically

Empowering your daughter to think critically is a crucial aspect of her development and growth. Critical thinking skills are essential for success in both academic and professional settings, as they allow individuals to analyze information, evaluate arguments, and make informed decisions. By encouraging your daughter to think critically, you are equipping her with the tools she needs to navigate complex issues, challenge assumptions, and develop innovative solutions.

One of the first steps in empowering your daughter to think critically is to encourage her curiosity and love of learning. Encourage her to ask questions, seek out new information, and explore different perspectives. By fostering a sense of curiosity, you are helping her develop a thirst for knowledge and a willingness to engage with challenging ideas. Encourage her to read widely, discuss ideas with others, and engage in activities that promote critical thinking, such as puzzles, debates, and research projects.

Another important aspect of empowering your daughter to think critically is teaching her to evaluate sources of information. In today's digital age, it is more important than ever for individuals to be able to discern fact from fiction and reliable sources from unreliable ones. Teach your daughter how to evaluate the credibility of sources, look for bias, and cross-check information. By equipping her with these skills, you are helping her become a discerning consumer of information and a responsible citizen.

Critical thinking also involves the ability to analyze arguments and think logically. Encourage your daughter to practice reasoning skills by engaging in debates, solving puzzles, and evaluating the strengths and weaknesses of different arguments. Help her develop a systematic approach to problem-solving, where she breaks down complex issues into smaller components and analyzes them systematically. By honing these skills, your daughter will be better equipped to make sound decisions and communicate her ideas effectively.

Empowering your daughter to think critically also means helping her develop a growth mindset. A growth mindset is the belief that abilities can be developed through hard work and dedication. By instilling this belief in your daughter, you are encouraging her to view challenges as opportunities for growth and learning. Help her see setbacks as temporary and opportunities to learn from mistakes. By fostering a growth mindset, you are empowering your daughter to persevere in the face of challenges and develop resilience.

In addition to fostering a growth mindset, it is also important to teach your daughter to embrace diversity and different perspectives. Encourage her to seek out perspectives that are different from her own, engage in discussions with people from diverse backgrounds, and challenge her assumptions. By exposing her to different viewpoints, you are helping her develop empathy, tolerance, and a deeper understanding of the world. Encourage her to engage with different cultures, learn new languages, and travel to new places. By doing so, you are broadening her perspective and equipping her with the tools she needs to think critically about complex issues. By fostering a sense of curiosity, teaching her to evaluate sources of information, honing her reasoning skills, instilling a growth mindset, and embracing diversity, you are equipping her with the tools she needs to navigate the complexities of the world and make informed decisions. Encourage her to engage with challenging ideas, seek out diverse perspectives, and develop innovative solutions. By empowering your daughter to think critically, you are setting her on a path to success in both academic and professional settings.

- Encouraging Positive Role Models for Your Daughter

Encouraging positive role models for your daughter is essential for her personal development and growth. Role models can have a significant impact on a young girl's self-esteem, confidence, and aspirations. By exposing your daughter to positive and influential individuals, you are not only providing her with inspiration but also setting the foundation for her to become a strong and empowered woman. In this article, we will discuss the importance of positive role models, how to identify them, and ways to encourage your daughter to look up to these individuals.

First and foremost, it is important to understand the power that role models hold in shaping a child's beliefs and attitudes. Children, especially girls, often look to adults or older individuals for guidance and inspiration. Positive role models can serve as examples of how to overcome adversity, achieve success, and lead a fulfilling life. By exposing your daughter to individuals who embody qualities such as perseverance, kindness, intelligence, and compassion, you are providing her with a roadmap for her own personal growth and development.

So how can you identify positive role models for your daughter. Start by looking within your own community and circle of acquaintances. Are there women in your life who inspire you with their work ethic, values, or achievements. These individuals can serve as excellent role models for your daughter. Additionally, consider seeking out women in positions of leadership or success in various fields, such as business, politics, science, or the arts. Show your daughter examples of women who have shattered stereotypes and glass ceilings, and emphasize the importance of hard work, determination, and resilience.

Once you have identified potential role models for your daughter, it is important to actively encourage her to look up to these individuals. Start by openly discussing the qualities and achievements of these role models with your daughter, and explain why they are worthy of admiration. Encourage your daughter to ask questions about these individuals and learn more about their backgrounds and accomplishments. Additionally, consider exposing your daughter to books, movies, or articles about these role models, so she can gain a deeper understanding of their stories and how they have impacted the world around them.

Furthermore, it is crucial to foster a supportive and nurturing environment that allows your daughter to explore her own interests and passions. Encourage her to pursue extracurricular activities or hobbies that spark her curiosity and creativity. Provide her with opportunities to meet other girls and women who share her interests and values, and who can serve as positive influences in her life. By surrounding your daughter with a diverse group of role models, she will be able to see the endless possibilities that are available to her and feel empowered to pursue her dreams. By exposing her to individuals who embody qualities such as resilience, kindness, intelligence, and leadership, you are setting the foundation for her to become a strong and empowered woman. Take the time to identify potential role models for your daughter, actively encourage her to learn more about their stories, and foster a supportive environment that allows her to explore her own interests and passions. By providing your daughter with positive influences and examples to look up to, you are helping her build the confidence and skills she needs to navigate the challenges of life and succeed in whatever she sets her mind to.

Chapter 9: Body Image and Self-Care

- PROMOTING A HEALTHY Body Image

Promoting a healthy body image is essential for overall well-being and mental health. Body image refers to how we see ourselves physically and how we feel about our bodies. In a society that puts a premium on physical appearance, it is easy to get caught up in unrealistic standards of beauty. This can lead to negative self-perception, low self-esteem, and even harmful behaviors such as disordered eating and excessive exercise. It is important to recognize that everyone is unique and that beauty comes in all shapes and sizes.

One way to promote a healthy body image is through positive self-talk. It is crucial to be kind to ourselves and to challenge negative thoughts about our bodies. Instead of focusing on perceived flaws or imperfections, we can choose to celebrate our strengths and embrace our bodies as they are. By practicing self-compassion and self-acceptance, we can cultivate a more positive and nurturing relationship with our bodies. This can help to improve self-esteem and overall well-being.

Another important aspect of promoting a healthy body image is to surround ourselves with positive influences. This includes engaging with media that celebrates diversity and representation of different body types. It is also helpful to spend time with individuals who appreciate us for who we are and support us in our journey towards self-acceptance. By creating a supportive environment, we can reinforce positive body image and counteract negative societal messages about beauty and worth.

Engaging in regular physical activity and nourishing our bodies with nutritious food is another key component of promoting a healthy body image. Exercise can help improve mood, increase energy levels, and enhance body confidence. By focusing on what our bodies can do rather than how they look, we can shift our mindset towards health and vitality. Eating a balanced diet that supports our physical and mental well-being is also important for cultivating a positive body image. Fueling our bodies with nutrient-rich foods can help us feel strong, energized, and comfortable in our own skin.

Seeking professional support and counseling can be beneficial for individuals struggling with body image issues. Therapists and counselors can help individuals explore underlying beliefs and emotions that contribute to negative self-perception. They can also provide tools and strategies for building self-esteem and developing a healthier body image. Additionally, support groups and online communities can offer a sense of belonging and solidarity for those navigating body image challenges. By reaching out for help and connecting with others who share similar experiences, individuals can feel less alone and more empowered in their journey towards self-acceptance. By embracing our uniqueness and celebrating our individuality, we can cultivate a more positive and empowering relationship with our bodies. It is important to remember that beauty comes in all shapes and sizes, and that true confidence and self-worth come from within. By taking small steps towards self-acceptance and self-care, we can foster a healthier body image and improve our overall well-being.

- Encouraging Self-Care Practices

Self-care practices are essential for overall well-being and quality of life. In today's fast-paced and stressful world, it is more important than ever to prioritize self-care in order to maintain physical, mental, and emotional health. Encouraging self-care practices is vital for individuals to take care of themselves and prevent burnout, exhaustion, and a decline in overall health. By understanding the importance of self-care and making it a priority in daily life, individuals can experience increased happiness, productivity, and resilience in the face of challenges.

Self-care encompasses a wide range of activities and behaviors that promote physical, mental, and emotional well-being. This includes practices such as exercise, healthy eating, sufficient rest, relaxation, mindfulness, and positive social connections. Each of these elements plays a crucial role in maintaining a balanced and healthy lifestyle. Regular physical activity, for example, not only improves physical health but also boosts mood and reduces stress levels. Similarly, eating a nutritious diet provides the body with essential nutrients for optimal functioning and can enhance overall well-being. Incorporating relaxation techniques such as deep breathing, meditation, or yoga can help create a sense of calm and reduce anxiety. Positive social connections and emotional support from friends and family can also provide a sense of belonging and support during difficult times.

Encouraging self-care practices involves promoting a balanced approach to life that prioritizes personal well-being. This means recognizing the importance of taking care of oneself in order to be able to effectively care for others and fulfill responsibilities. It also involves setting aside time and energy for self-care activities, even in the midst of a busy schedule. By making self-care a priority, individuals can prevent burnout and improve their overall quality of life. This can lead to increased productivity, better relationships, and a greater sense of fulfillment.

One way to encourage self-care practices is to create a supportive environment that values and promotes well-being. This can be done through policies and practices that prioritize work-life balance, stress management, and mental health support. Employers, for example, can offer flexible work arrangements, mental health resources, and wellness programs to support employees in taking care of themselves. Schools and community organizations can also promote self-care through education and awareness campaigns that emphasize the importance of self-care practices. By creating a culture that values self-care, individuals are more likely to prioritize their own well-being and make time for self-care activities.

Another way to encourage self-care practices is to provide resources and tools that support individuals in taking care of themselves. This can include access to information about self-care practices, online resources, self-help books, and workshops or classes on self-care techniques. By providing individuals with the knowledge and tools they need to practice self-care, they are more likely to incorporate these practices into their daily routine. It is also important to destigmatize self-care and mental health issues in order to create a supportive environment where individuals feel comfortable seeking help and prioritizing their well-being. By normalizing self-care practices and promoting a culture of well-being, individuals can feel empowered to take care of themselves and improve their overall quality of life. By prioritizing self-care and making it a regular part of daily life, individuals can experience increased happiness, productivity, and resilience in the face of challenges. It is important to recognize the value of self-care practices and create a supportive environment that values and promotes well-being. By providing resources and tools that support individuals in taking care of themselves, we can help individuals prioritize their own well-being and improve their overall quality of life. Self-care is not selfish, but rather an essential practice for maintaining physical, mental, and emotional health. Let us all prioritize self-care and encourage others to do the same in order to live a happier, healthier, and more fulfilling life.

- Addressing Eating Disorders and Body Dysmorphia

Eating disorders and body dysmorphia are complex mental health conditions that can have serious consequences for an individual's physical and emotional well-being. It is important for individuals struggling with these issues to seek help from a qualified healthcare professional, as early intervention can greatly improve the chances of recovery. In this essay, we will discuss the causes, symptoms, and treatment options for eating disorders and body dysmorphia, as well as strategies for prevention and recovery.

Eating disorders are mental health conditions that are characterized by unhealthy eating habits and a preoccupation with weight and body image. The three most common types of eating disorders are anorexia nervosa, bulimia nervosa, and binge eating disorder. Anorexia nervosa is characterized by extreme calorie restriction and a fear of gaining weight, often leading to dangerously low body weight. Bulimia nervosa involves binge eating followed by purging behaviors, such as vomiting or using laxatives, to compensate for the calorie intake. Binge eating disorder is characterized by recurrent episodes of binge eating without compensatory behaviors.

Body dysmorphia, also known as body dysmorphic disorder, is a mental health condition in which individuals have a distorted perception of their own appearance. They may be excessively concerned about perceived flaws or defects in their appearance, which can cause significant distress and impair their daily functioning. Body dysmorphia can lead to obsessive thoughts and compulsive behaviors related to appearance, such as constantly checking the mirror or seeking cosmetic procedures to correct perceived flaws.

The exact causes of eating disorders and body dysmorphia are not fully understood, but they are believed to be a combination of genetic, psychological, and environmental factors. Genetics may play a role in predisposing individuals to these conditions, as they tend to run in families. Psychological factors, such as low self-esteem, perfectionism, and a history of trauma or abuse, can also contribute to the development of eating disorders and body dysmorphia. Environmental factors, such as societal pressures to conform to a certain standard of beauty or diet culture, can also influence the development of these conditions.

The symptoms of eating disorders and body dysmorphia vary depending on the individual and the specific condition. Common symptoms of anorexia nervosa include severe weight loss, preoccupation with food and calories, distorted body image, and excessive exercise. Symptoms of bulimia nervosa may include binge eating episodes, purging behaviors, and feelings of guilt or shame about eating. Binge eating disorder is characterized by recurrent episodes of binge eating without compensatory behaviors, leading to feelings of guilt and distress. Symptoms of body dysmorphia include obsessive thoughts about perceived flaws in appearance, avoidance of mirrors or social situations, and seeking reassurance about one's appearance.

Treatment for eating disorders and body dysmorphia typically involves a multidisciplinary approach, which may include therapy, medication, nutritional counseling, and support groups. Cognitive-behavioral therapy (CBT) is often used to help individuals challenge negative thoughts and behaviors related to body image and food. Medication, such as antidepressants or anti-anxiety medications, may be prescribed to help manage symptoms of anxiety or depression. Nutritional counseling can help individuals develop a healthy relationship with food and learn to nourish their bodies appropriately. Support groups can provide a sense of community and understanding for individuals struggling with eating disorders and body dysmorphia.

Prevention of eating disorders and body dysmorphia involves promoting positive body image and self-esteem, challenging societal pressures to conform to a certain standard of beauty, and encouraging healthy eating habits. Parents, educators, and healthcare professionals can play a crucial role in promoting body positivity and self-acceptance in children and adolescents. Teaching individuals to have a healthy relationship with food and exercise, rather than focusing on restrictive dieting or extreme exercise regimens, can also help prevent the development of eating disorders and body dysmorphia. Encouraging open communication about body image and self-esteem can help individuals feel supported and understood. Individuals struggling with these issues should seek support from a qualified healthcare professional to receive a comprehensive assessment and personalized treatment plan. With early intervention and appropriate treatment, individuals can overcome eating disorders and body dysmorphia and regain a healthy relationship with food and their bodies. Prevention efforts should focus on promoting positive body image, self-esteem, and healthy eating habits to reduce the risk of developing these conditions. By raising awareness and providing support, we can help individuals struggling with eating disorders and body dysmorphia on their journey to recovery and healing.

Chapter 10: Academic and Career Guidance

- SUPPORTING YOUR DAUGHTER'S Educational Journey

Supporting your daughter's educational journey is crucial to her success and development. As a parent, you play a key role in helping her navigate the challenges and opportunities that come with pursuing an education. By providing her with the necessary tools, resources, and guidance, you can empower her to excel academically and reach her full potential. In this article, we will explore some practical strategies and tips on how you can support your daughter's educational journey and create a positive learning environment for her.

One of the most important ways you can support your daughter's educational journey is by being actively involved in her academic life. This means taking an interest in her schoolwork, attending parent-teacher conferences, and communicating regularly with her teachers. By staying informed about her progress and performance in school, you can better understand her strengths and weaknesses and provide the necessary support and encouragement. Additionally, being actively involved in her education shows her that you value her learning and are committed to helping her succeed.

Another important aspect of supporting your daughter's educational journey is creating a conducive and supportive learning environment at home. This includes setting aside a designated study space, establishing a consistent routine for homework and study time, and providing access to necessary resources such as textbooks, supplies, and technology. By creating a structured and organized environment for your daughter to study in, you can help her stay focused and motivated to learn.

In addition to providing a supportive learning environment at home, it is also important to encourage your daughter to take ownership of her education. This means fostering a sense of responsibility and independence in her academic pursuits, and empowering her to set goals, manage her time effectively, and advocate for herself when needed. By teaching her these essential skills, you can help her develop a strong sense of self-reliance and resilience that will serve her well in her educational journey and beyond.

One effective way to support your daughter's educational journey is to actively engage with her in discussions about her academic interests, goals, and aspirations. Encourage her to share her thoughts and ideas with you, and listen attentively to her concerns and challenges. By having open and honest conversations with your daughter about her education, you can better understand her needs and preferences, and provide the necessary guidance and support to help her succeed.

Furthermore, it is important to recognize and celebrate your daughter's achievements and milestones along her educational journey. Whether she receives an award, achieves a high grade on a test, or completes a challenging project, make sure to acknowledge and praise her efforts. By recognizing and celebrating her accomplishments, you can boost her confidence and motivation, and help her develop a positive attitude towards learning.

In addition to providing academic support, it is also important to prioritize your daughter's overall well-being and mental health. Help her develop healthy study habits and coping mechanisms for managing stress, and encourage her to maintain a balance between schoolwork and leisure activities. By promoting a healthy work-life balance for your daughter, you can help her avoid burnout and sustain her motivation and enthusiasm for learning.

Lastly, it is essential to create a supportive network of resources and opportunities for your daughter to enhance her educational journey. This may include enrolling her in extracurricular activities, providing access to tutoring services or academic enrichment programs, and connecting her with mentors or role models in her field of interest. By exposing your daughter to a diverse range of learning experiences and opportunities, you can help her expand her horizons, discover her passions, and cultivate a lifelong love for learning. By being actively involved in her academic life, creating a conducive learning environment at home, empowering her to take ownership of her education, engaging in open and honest conversations about her academic interests, goals, and challenges, recognizing and celebrating her achievements, prioritizing her well-being and mental health, and providing a supportive network of resources and opportunities, you can help your daughter thrive academically and reach her full potential. Remember, your support and encouragement are invaluable in shaping your daughter's educational journey and preparing her for a successful and fulfilling future.

- Exploring Career Options and Goals

Exploring career options and setting professional goals are essential steps in achieving success and fulfillment in one's chosen field. It is important to take the time to carefully consider the various career paths available and to identify the goals that will ultimately guide your career trajectory. This process involves self-reflection, research, and strategic planning. By exploring different career options and setting clear goals, individuals can create a roadmap for their professional development and ensure that they are making informed decisions about their future.

One of the first steps in exploring career options is to conduct a self-assessment to identify your interests, skills, values, and personality traits. This can help you gain a better understanding of who you are and what you want out of a career. By taking the time to reflect on your strengths and weaknesses, you can begin to identify potential career paths that align with your interests and abilities. Additionally, it is important to consider your values and what is important to you in a career, such as work-life balance, opportunities for growth and advancement, and the ability to make a meaningful impact.

Once you have completed a self-assessment, the next step is to research different career options that align with your interests and goals. This may involve exploring industries, job roles, and organizations that appeal to you. Conducting informational interviews with professionals in your field of interest can provide valuable insights into what a particular career entails and what it takes to be successful in that role. Additionally, attending networking events, job fairs, and industry conferences can help you expand your professional network and learn more about the opportunities available in your desired field.

Setting specific, measurable, achievable, relevant, and time-bound (SMART) goals is essential in guiding your career development and ensuring that you are making progress toward your objectives. When setting career goals, it is important to consider both short-term and long-term objectives. Short-term goals may include gaining specific skills, completing a certification or degree program, or securing a relevant internship or job opportunity. Long-term goals, on the other hand, may involve advancing to a higher position within your chosen field, starting your own business, or making a career transition to a different industry.

It is important to regularly review and adjust your career goals as needed to ensure that they remain relevant and realistic. As you gain new experiences, skills, and insights, your career interests and priorities may evolve, requiring you to revise your goals accordingly. By regularly evaluating your progress and updating your goals, you can stay on track and make informed decisions about your career path. By conducting a self-assessment, researching different career options, and setting SMART goals, individuals can develop a clear roadmap for their professional development. Regularly reviewing and adjusting career goals as needed can help ensure that they remain relevant and aligned with one's evolving interests and priorities. Ultimately, by taking the time to explore career options and set clear goals, individuals can position themselves for success and fulfillment in their chosen field.

- Empowering Your Daughter to Pursue her Dreams

As parents, one of the most important roles we have is to empower our daughters to pursue their dreams. In a world that is constantly changing and evolving, it is essential that we instill in our daughters the belief that they can achieve anything they set their minds to. By providing them with the tools, support, and encouragement they need, we can help them navigate the challenges they will undoubtedly face as they chase their goals.

One of the key ways we can empower our daughters is by fostering a sense of self-confidence and self-worth. We must teach them to believe in themselves and their abilities, and to never let anyone else define their worth. Encouraging our daughters to take risks and step outside of their comfort zones is crucial in helping them build resilience and develop the confidence to pursue their dreams. By praising their efforts and achievements, no matter how big or small, we can boost their self-esteem and motivate them to keep pushing forward.

Another important aspect of empowering our daughters is providing them with access to education and opportunities. We must encourage them to excel academically and pursue their interests and passions. By supporting and nurturing their intellectual curiosity, we can help them develop the skills and knowledge they need to succeed in any field they choose. Additionally, we must expose them to a variety of experiences and encourage them to explore different career paths, so they can make informed decisions about their future.

It is also essential that we teach our daughters to advocate for themselves and stand up for what they believe in. They must learn to speak their minds and assert their opinions, even in the face of opposition. By teaching them to be assertive and assertive, we can help them develop the confidence and courage to pursue their dreams. We must also teach them the importance of resilience and perseverance, as obstacles and setbacks are inevitable on the path to success. By helping them develop a growth mindset and a positive attitude towards failure, we can empower them to bounce back stronger and more determined than ever.

In addition to providing our daughters with the skills and support they need to pursue their dreams, we must also be role models for them. We must show them what it means to be strong, independent, and determined, and inspire them to be the best versions of themselves. By demonstrating resilience, perseverance, and a passion for learning, we can set an example for our daughters to follow. We must also be open and honest with them about our own successes and failures, so they can learn from our experiences and be inspired to overcome their own challenges.

Ultimately, empowering our daughters to pursue their dreams is about giving them the confidence, skills, and support they need to thrive in a rapidly changing world. By instilling in them a belief in themselves and their abilities, providing them with access to education and opportunities, teaching them to advocate for themselves, and being role models for them, we can help them achieve their goals and reach their full potential. It may not always be easy, but with love, encouragement, and unwavering support, we can empower our daughters to conquer any obstacle and make their dreams a reality.

Chapter 11: Encouraging Independence and Autonomy

- BALANCING SUPPORT and Freedom

Balancing support and freedom is a fundamental aspect of any healthy and functional relationship, whether it be between parents and children, teachers and students, or managers and employees. This delicate equilibrium is essential for fostering trust, autonomy, and growth in individuals while also providing a safety net and guidance when needed. In order to strike the right balance between offering support and allowing for freedom, it is crucial to understand the unique needs and preferences of each party involved, as well as the larger context and goals of the relationship.

Support can come in many forms, including emotional support, practical assistance, and guidance or advice. It is about being there for someone in times of need, providing a listening ear, and offering help or resources to overcome challenges. Support is essential for fostering resilience, self-esteem, and a sense of security in individuals, enabling them to take risks, learn from mistakes, and ultimately thrive. However, too much support can stifle independence, creativity, and personal growth, leading to dependence and a lack of initiative.

On the other hand, freedom is about allowing individuals to make their own choices, take risks, and explore their interests and abilities without undue interference or control. It is about respecting their autonomy, values, and preferences, and trusting them to make decisions that are in their best interests. Freedom is essential for fostering self-confidence, motivation, and a sense of ownership in individuals, enabling them to develop a strong sense of identity and purpose. However, too much freedom can lead to chaos, confusion, and a lack of direction, as individuals may struggle to make decisions or take responsibility for their actions.

Finding the right balance between support and freedom requires a nuanced and flexible approach that takes into account the specific needs and circumstances of each individual or group. It involves creating a supportive and nurturing environment that allows for freedom of expression, experimentation, and growth, while also providing structure, guidance, and boundaries to ensure safety and well-being. It requires clear communication, mutual respect, and empathy, as well as a willingness to adapt and compromise when necessary.

One way to balance support and freedom is by setting clear expectations, boundaries, and goals, while also allowing for flexibility, creativity, and spontaneity. This involves creating a supportive and empowering atmosphere where individuals feel valued, respected, and understood, while also being challenged to push their limits and discover their full potential. It requires striking a balance between nurturing and challenging, protecting and empowering, guiding and letting go, in order to create a dynamic and harmonious relationship that fosters growth, collaboration, and mutual respect.

Another way to balance support and freedom is by fostering a culture of trust, open communication, and collaboration, where individuals feel safe, empowered, and encouraged to express themselves, take risks, and learn from their experiences. This involves cultivating a sense of belonging, connection, and mutual support, while also encouraging autonomy, creativity, and agency. It requires building strong relationships based on honesty, transparency, and mutual respect, as well as creating a shared vision, purpose, and values that guide and inspire individuals to work together towards common goals and aspirations.

- Fostering Decision-Making Skills

Decision-making is a crucial skill that is essential in both our personal and professional lives. It involves the process of selecting a course of action from multiple options based on careful consideration of the available information. In today's fast-paced and complex world, the ability to make effective decisions is more important than ever. Therefore, it is crucial to foster decision-making skills to navigate through the myriad of choices and challenges that we face on a daily basis.

One of the key aspects of fostering decision-making skills is developing critical thinking abilities. Critical thinking involves the ability to analyze information objectively, evaluate different perspectives, and draw logical s. By honing their critical thinking skills, individuals can make more informed and thoughtful decisions. This can be achieved through activities such as engaging in debates, solving complex problems, or critically evaluating information sources. By challenging their own assumptions and expanding their perspectives, individuals can enhance their ability to make sound decisions.

Another important aspect of fostering decision-making skills is developing emotional intelligence. Emotional intelligence involves the ability to recognize and manage one's own emotions, as well as understand and empathize with the emotions of others. Emotions play a significant role in the decision-making process, as they can influence our judgment and behavior. By developing emotional intelligence, individuals can better regulate their emotions and make decisions that are not solely based on impulse or bias. This can be achieved through practices such as mindfulness, self-reflection, and empathy training. By increasing their emotional intelligence, individuals can make decisions that are more aligned with their values and goals.

Furthermore, fostering decision-making skills involves developing problem-solving abilities. Problem-solving skills are essential for identifying and addressing challenges effectively. This involves breaking down complex issues into smaller, more manageable parts, generating creative solutions, and implementing them in a systematic manner. By honing their problem-solving abilities, individuals can navigate through obstacles and make decisions that are practical and sustainable. This can be achieved through activities such as brainstorming sessions, role-playing exercises, and case studies. By practicing problem-solving skills, individuals can enhance their decision-making capabilities and adapt to changing circumstances.

Additionally, fostering decision-making skills requires creating a supportive learning environment. This involves encouraging open communication, collaboration, and feedback among individuals. By fostering a culture of learning and growth, individuals can feel empowered to take risks, experiment with new ideas, and learn from their mistakes. This can be achieved through practices such as team-building activities, group discussions, and peer evaluations. By creating a supportive learning environment, individuals can feel more confident in their decision-making abilities and be more open to trying new approaches. This can lead to a more innovative and dynamic decision-making process. By developing critical thinking abilities, emotional intelligence, problem-solving skills, and creating a supportive learning environment, individuals can enhance their decision-making capabilities and make informed and thoughtful choices. It is important to continually practice and refine these skills through continuous learning and self-improvement. By fostering decision-making skills, individuals can become more effective leaders, problem-solvers, and innovators in today's rapidly changing world.

- Allowing Your Daughter to Learn from Mistakes

Allowing your daughter to learn from mistakes is a crucial aspect of her development and growth. As parents, it can be tempting to shield our children from failure and disappointment, thinking that it will protect them from harm or disappointment. However, research has shown that allowing children to make mistakes and learn from them is actually beneficial for their overall development and self-esteem. By allowing your daughter to experience failure, you are giving her the opportunity to build resilience, problem-solving skills, and self-confidence.

One of the key benefits of allowing your daughter to learn from mistakes is that it helps her develop resilience. Resilience is the ability to bounce back from setbacks and challenges, and it is a crucial skill that will serve her well throughout her life. When children are shielded from failure and never allowed to make mistakes, they do not have the opportunity to learn how to cope with disappointment and setbacks. By allowing your daughter to experience failure, you are giving her the chance to develop resilience and learn how to overcome obstacles.

In addition to building resilience, allowing your daughter to learn from mistakes also helps her develop problem-solving skills. When children are faced with failure, they are forced to think creatively and come up with solutions to overcome the challenges they are facing. By allowing your daughter to make mistakes and learn from them, you are helping her develop critical thinking skills and the ability to find solutions to problems on her own. This will serve her well not only in her academic and professional life but also in her personal relationships.

Furthermore, allowing your daughter to make mistakes and learn from them helps build her self-confidence. When children are constantly shielded from failure, they may begin to doubt their abilities and develop a fear of making mistakes. By allowing your daughter to experience failure and learn from it, you are showing her that it is okay to make mistakes and that failure is a natural part of the learning process. This will help her develop a growth mindset and a positive attitude towards challenges and setbacks.

It is important to remember that allowing your daughter to learn from mistakes does not mean abandoning her or leaving her to fend for herself. As a parent, it is your job to provide support and guidance while still allowing her to experience failure and learn from it. Encourage her to reflect on her mistakes, identify what went wrong, and come up with a plan to do better next time. Offer your support and encouragement as she navigates through the learning process, and be there to celebrate her successes and offer comfort during moments of disappointment. By giving her the opportunity to experience failure and learn from it, you are helping her build resilience, problem-solving skills, and self-confidence. Remember to provide support and guidance as she navigates through the learning process and be there to celebrate her successes and offer comfort during moments of disappointment. By allowing your daughter to make mistakes and learn from them, you are helping her develop the skills and mindset she needs to thrive in all areas of her life.

Chapter 12: Creating Shared Experiences and Memories

- STRENGTHENING THE Parent-Daughter Bond

The parent-daughter bond is a crucial aspect of family relationships that can greatly impact a child's development and well-being. Strengthening this bond is essential for fostering a sense of trust, support, and connection between parents and their daughters. Research has shown that strong parent-daughter relationships can have a positive impact on a child's emotional, social, and cognitive development. When parents and daughters have a close and supportive relationship, it can lead to better communication, increased self-esteem, and a greater sense of security for the child.

There are several key ways in which parents can strengthen the bond with their daughters. First and foremost, communication is key. Parents should strive to have open and honest conversations with their daughters, listening to their concerns, thoughts, and feelings with empathy and understanding. By creating a safe space for dialogue, parents can foster a sense of trust and intimacy with their daughters. It is important for parents to actively listen to their daughters, validate their emotions, and offer guidance and support when needed.

In addition to fostering open communication, parents can strengthen the bond with their daughters by spending quality time together. Shared activities and experiences can help build connections and create lasting memories. Whether it's taking a walk in the park, cooking a meal together, or engaging in a hobby or sport that both parent and daughter enjoy, spending time together can strengthen the bond between parent and child. Doing activities that allow for collaboration and teamwork can also help foster a sense of connection and mutual respect between parents and daughters.

Another important aspect of strengthening the parent-daughter bond is showing love and affection. Parents should express their love for their daughters through both words and actions. Simple gestures like a hug, a kind word, or a thoughtful gesture can go a long way in showing daughters that they are loved and valued. Parents should also make an effort to show appreciation for their daughters' strengths, talents, and accomplishments, and provide encouragement and support when they face challenges or setbacks. By showing love and affirmation, parents can help build their daughters' self-esteem and confidence.

It is also important for parents to set boundaries and establish clear expectations for their daughters. Boundaries help to create a sense of security and structure in the parent-daughter relationship, while expectations provide guidance and direction. Parents should communicate their expectations clearly and consistently, and hold their daughters accountable for their actions and behaviors. By setting boundaries and expectations, parents can help their daughters develop a sense of responsibility, respect, and self-discipline.

In addition to these strategies, parents can also help strengthen the parent-daughter bond by being positive role models. Parents should strive to demonstrate healthy communication, conflict resolution, and problem-solving skills in their own relationships, serving as a model for their daughters to follow. By showing respect, empathy, and kindness in their interactions with others, parents can teach their daughters important values and skills that can help strengthen their own relationships in the future. By fostering open communication, spending quality time together, showing love and affection, setting boundaries and expectations, and being positive role models, parents can help build a strong and healthy relationship with their daughters that can have a lasting impact on their well-being and development. It is important for parents to prioritize their relationship with their daughters and invest time and effort into building a strong and supportive bond that will benefit both parent and child for years to come.

- Building Traditions and Rituals

Traditions and rituals are an essential part of human culture and society. They serve as a way for people to connect with their past, create a sense of belonging, and establish a sense of continuity and stability in their lives. Building traditions and rituals within a family, community, or organization can have a profound impact on the members involved, providing them with a sense of identity and purpose.

Traditions are customs or beliefs that are passed down from generation to generation. They can take many forms, ranging from religious practices to holiday celebrations to family rituals. Traditions often involve specific actions, symbols, or ceremonies that hold deep meaning for those who participate in them. They provide a sense of continuity and connection with the past, allowing individuals to feel connected to their ancestors and heritage.

Rituals, on the other hand, are a specific type of tradition that involves a series of actions or behaviors performed in a prescribed manner. Rituals often have a symbolic significance and are used to mark important events or transitions in life. They can be personal, such as a daily meditation practice, or communal, such as a wedding ceremony or graduation ceremony. Rituals help to create a sense of structure and order in our lives, providing a sense of comfort and predictability in an uncertain world.

Building traditions and rituals within a family can be a powerful way to strengthen bonds between family members and create a sense of unity. Family traditions can include things like holiday celebrations, annual vacations, or weekly family dinners. These rituals provide opportunities for family members to come together, share experiences, and create lasting memories. They also serve to pass down values, beliefs, and customs from one generation to the next, helping to preserve the family's heritage and traditions.

In a community or organization, traditions and rituals can play a similar role in creating a sense of connection and belonging among members. Community traditions might include local festivals, cultural celebrations, or annual events that bring people together. These traditions can help to foster a sense of pride and identity among community members, as well as promote unity and cooperation. In organizations, rituals such as weekly team meetings, annual retreats, or recognition ceremonies can help to build camaraderie among employees and reinforce the values and mission of the organization.

It is important to note that traditions and rituals are not static or unchanging. They can evolve over time to reflect the changing needs and values of a society or group. For example, a family might adapt its holiday traditions to accommodate new family members or changing circumstances. Similarly, an organization might update its rituals to align with its evolving goals and objectives. By maintaining flexibility and openness to change, traditions and rituals can continue to serve their intended purpose of creating connection and meaning for those who participate in them. Whether within a family, community, or organization, traditions and rituals provide a sense of continuity, identity, and belonging. By honoring and preserving the customs and practices that hold meaning for us, we can create a sense of shared history and purpose that can be passed down to future generations. By embracing traditions and rituals with openness and creativity, we can continue to build strong bonds and create meaningful experiences that enrich our lives.

- Making Time for Quality Time Together

In today's fast-paced world, it can be challenging to find the time to spend with loved ones. However, making time for quality time together is essential for nurturing relationships and maintaining emotional connections. Quality time is not just about being physically present, but about being fully engaged and present in the moment. It is about showing genuine interest, listening actively, and creating meaningful experiences together.

One of the first steps in making time for quality time together is recognizing the importance of prioritizing it in our busy schedules. It can be all too easy to get caught up in work, chores, and other responsibilities, but it is crucial to carve out time for our relationships. This may mean setting aside specific blocks of time each day or week to spend with loved ones, whether it be a family dinner, a movie night, or a weekend getaway. By consciously prioritizing quality time, we can strengthen our bonds with those we care about most.

Another key aspect of making time for quality time together is being intentional about how we spend that time. Rather than simply being in the same room or going through the motions, it is important to actively engage with one another and create memorable experiences. This may involve planning activities that everyone enjoys, such as cooking a meal together, going for a hike, or playing a board game. By focusing on shared experiences and meaningful interactions, we can make the most of our time together and deepen our connections.

Communication is also vital when it comes to making time for quality time together. It is important to openly communicate with loved ones about our needs, preferences, and expectations for spending time together. By having honest conversations and setting clear boundaries, we can ensure that everyone feels valued and respected. Communication can also help us make the most of our time together by expressing our thoughts and feelings, sharing stories and memories, and building stronger connections with those we care about.

In addition to prioritizing quality time with loved ones, it is also important to take care of ourselves and prioritize self-care. By making time for activities that recharge and rejuvenate us, we can show up as our best selves in our relationships. This may involve practicing mindfulness, engaging in hobbies we enjoy, or simply taking time to relax and unwind. By prioritizing self-care, we can improve our overall well-being and have more to give to our loved ones when we are together.

Ultimately, making time for quality time together is a choice that we must actively make in our daily lives. It requires conscious effort, communication, and intentionality to prioritize our relationships and create meaningful experiences with loved ones. By recognizing the importance of quality time, being intentional about how we spend that time, communicating openly with one another, and prioritizing self-care, we can strengthen our bonds with loved ones and cultivate deeper connections that will last a lifetime.

Chapter 13: Addressing Gender Stereotypes and Bias

- CHALLENGING GENDER Norms and Expectations

Gender norms and expectations have long been ingrained in societies around the world, dictating how individuals should behave based on their perceived gender. These norms often limit individuals' potential and reinforce harmful stereotypes. Challenging these norms is essential to promoting gender equality and creating a more inclusive and diverse society. By breaking down these traditional expectations, we can create space for individuals to express themselves authentically and without fear of judgment or discrimination.

One common gender norm that is often challenged is the idea that women should be nurturing and caring, while men should be strong and aggressive. This binary view of gender roles can be harmful as it limits individuals' ability to fully express themselves and can lead to feelings of inadequacy or alienation. By challenging this norm, we can create a more inclusive society where individuals are free to explore and embrace different aspects of their personality without fear of judgment. This can lead to increased personal fulfillment and a sense of belonging for all individuals, regardless of their gender identity.

Another prevalent gender norm that is often challenged is the idea that individuals should conform to traditional gender presentations based on their assigned sex at birth. This norm often results in discrimination against individuals who do not fit into these narrow categories, such as transgender and gender non-conforming individuals. By challenging this norm, we can create a society that is more accepting and affirming of diverse gender expressions.

This can lead to increased visibility and representation for marginalized communities, ultimately leading to a more equitable and just society for all.

Challenging gender norms and expectations requires a concerted effort from individuals, communities, and institutions. Education and awareness are key components in this process, as they can help to dismantle harmful stereotypes and promote a more inclusive understanding of gender. By engaging in open and honest conversations about gender norms, we can create a culture that is more accepting and affirming of diverse identities. This can help to break down barriers that prevent individuals from fully expressing themselves and living authentically.

In addition to education and awareness, challenging gender norms also requires individuals to take action and advocate for change. This can involve supporting policies and initiatives that promote gender equality and diversity, as well as actively challenging discriminatory practices and beliefs. By working together to challenge harmful gender norms, we can create a more inclusive and equitable society for all individuals, regardless of their gender identity or expression.

Ultimately, challenging gender norms and expectations is essential for promoting gender equality and creating a more inclusive and diverse society. By breaking down these traditional expectations, we can create space for individuals to express themselves authentically and without fear of judgment or discrimination. Through education, awareness, and advocacy, we can work together to challenge harmful stereotypes and promote a more inclusive understanding of gender. This can lead to increased personal fulfillment and a sense of belonging for all individuals, ultimately creating a more equitable and just society for all.

- Empowering Your Daughter to Define her Own Identity

Empowering daughters to define their own identity is a crucial aspect of parenting in today's world. In a society that often imposes rigid gender roles and expectations on individuals, it is important for parents to support their daughters in exploring and embracing their true selves. By encouraging them to define their own identity, parents can help their daughters develop a strong sense of self-worth and confidence that will serve them well throughout their lives.

One of the key ways to empower your daughter to define her own identity is to create a supportive and nurturing environment at home. This means being open and accepting of her thoughts, feelings, and interests, and providing her with the freedom to express herself without fear of judgment or criticism. By fostering a sense of safety and trust in the home, parents can help their daughters feel comfortable exploring different aspects of their identity and developing a sense of who they are and who they want to be.

Another important aspect of empowering daughters to define their own identity is to be a positive role model. Parents can demonstrate the value of self-acceptance and self-expression by being true to themselves and living authentically. By showing their daughters that it is okay to be different and unique, parents can help them embrace their own individuality and set an example for how to navigate the complexities of identity in a world that often tries to confine individuals to narrow stereotypes and labels.

In addition to creating a supportive environment and being a positive role model, parents can also empower their daughters to define their own identity by encouraging them to explore their interests and passions. This means providing opportunities for daughters to pursue activities and hobbies that resonate with them, whether it be sports, art, music, or academic pursuits. By supporting their daughters in following their passions, parents can help them develop a sense of purpose and fulfillment that will contribute to a strong and resilient sense of self.

It is also important for parents to have open and honest conversations with their daughters about identity and self-expression. This includes discussing topics such as gender, sexuality, race, and culture, and helping daughters navigate the complexities of these aspects of their identity. By having these conversations in a supportive and non-judgmental way, parents can help their daughters develop a nuanced and inclusive understanding of identity that will serve them well as they navigate the challenges of adolescence and young adulthood.

Ultimately, empowering daughters to define their own identity is about giving them the tools and support they need to navigate the complexities of self-discovery and self-expression. By creating a supportive and nurturing environment, being positive role models, encouraging exploration and passion, and fostering open and honest conversations, parents can help their daughters embrace their true selves and develop a strong sense of identity that will serve them well throughout their lives. By empowering daughters to define their own identity, parents can help them navigate the challenges of growing up in a world that often imposes rigid expectations and stereotypes, and empower them to live authentically and confidently as they navigate the complexities of adolescence and young adulthood.

- Promoting Gender Equality and Inclusivity

Promoting gender equality and inclusivity is a crucial aspect of creating a more equitable and just society. In recent years, there has been a growing recognition of the need to address issues of discrimination and bias based on gender. Gender equality is not just a matter of ensuring equal rights and opportunities for all individuals, regardless of their gender identity. It is also about challenging and dismantling the harmful stereotypes and norms that contribute to the marginalization of certain groups within society.

One of the key ways to promote gender equality and inclusivity is through education and awareness-raising efforts. By educating individuals about the importance of gender equality and the ways in which gender discrimination can manifest in society, we can help to change attitudes and beliefs that perpetuate inequality. This can involve providing training and resources to teachers, students, and community members, as well as implementing policies and programs that promote gender equality in schools and workplaces.

Another important aspect of promoting gender equality and inclusivity is ensuring that women and other marginalized groups have equal access to opportunities and resources. This can involve implementing policies that address pay equity, ensuring that women have equal access to leadership positions and decision-making roles, and providing support services for those who have experienced discrimination or violence based on their gender identity. By addressing these systemic barriers, we can help to create a more equal and inclusive society for all individuals.

In addition to education and access to opportunities, it is also important to create spaces and communities that are inclusive and welcoming to individuals of all genders. This can involve creating safe and supportive environments for individuals who may be at risk of discrimination or violence based on their gender identity, as well as promoting diversity and inclusivity within organizations and communities. By celebrating and valuing the contributions of individuals of all genders, we can help to create a more inclusive and equitable society for everyone.

Promoting gender equality and inclusivity is not just a matter of individual behavior or attitudes. It also involves challenging and changing the structural inequalities and biases that exist within society. This can involve advocating for changes to laws and policies that perpetuate discrimination, as well as working to dismantle systems of oppression and privilege that disadvantage certain groups based on their gender identity. By addressing these broader issues, we can help to create a more equitable and just society for all individuals, regardless of their gender identity. By educating individuals, ensuring equal access to opportunities, creating inclusive spaces and communities, and addressing structural inequalities and biases, we can help to create a society that values and respects individuals of all genders. It is important for all individuals to be engaged in this work and to actively challenge discrimination and bias wherever it may exist. By working together to promote gender equality and inclusivity, we can help to create a society that is more just, equitable, and inclusive for all.

Chapter 14: Resolving Conflict and Managing Differences

- STRATEGIES FOR EFFECTIVE Conflict Resolution

Conflict is an inevitable part of human interaction, whether in personal relationships, professional settings, or societal dynamics. Effective conflict resolution is essential for maintaining healthy relationships, fostering team cohesion, and promoting organizational productivity. In this article, we will delve into strategies for effectively managing conflict, exploring various approaches and techniques that can help individuals navigate disagreements and reach mutually beneficial resolutions.

One of the key strategies for effective conflict resolution is communication. Clear and open communication is essential for understanding the perspectives of all parties involved, identifying the root causes of the conflict, and working towards a solution. Active listening plays a crucial role in effective communication, as it allows individuals to fully grasp the concerns and emotions of the other party. By actively listening and demonstrating empathy, individuals can create a safe and supportive environment for resolving conflicts collaboratively.

Another important strategy for effective conflict resolution is maintaining a calm and respectful demeanor. Emotions can run high during conflicts, leading to irrational behavior and escalating tensions. By remaining composed and respectful, individuals can create a conducive atmosphere for constructive dialogue and negotiation. It is essential to avoid personal attacks and focus on addressing the issues at hand in a professional manner. By showing respect towards others, individuals can build trust and credibility, which are essential for successful conflict resolution.

Collaboration and compromise are also vital components of effective conflict resolution. Instead of approaching conflicts as win-lose situations, individuals should strive for win-win outcomes that meet the needs and interests of all parties involved. Collaborative problem-solving involves acknowledging and valuing the perspectives of others, seeking common ground, and exploring creative solutions that address everyone's concerns. By working together towards a mutually beneficial resolution, individuals can build stronger relationships and foster a sense of unity and cooperation.

Another effective strategy for conflict resolution is conflict coaching. Conflict coaching involves working with a neutral third party, such as a mediator or facilitator, to help individuals navigate conflicts and find mutually acceptable solutions. Conflict coaches can provide valuable insights, guidance, and support to help individuals better understand the dynamics of the conflict, identify their underlying interests and concerns, and explore alternative approaches for resolving the dispute. By seeking the assistance of a conflict coach, individuals can gain new perspectives, develop effective communication skills, and reach sustainable resolutions that address the root causes of the conflict.

It is also essential to recognize the importance of emotional intelligence in conflict resolution. Emotional intelligence refers to the ability to identify, assess, and manage one's own emotions and the emotions of others. By being aware of their emotions and those of others, individuals can better regulate their reactions during conflicts, communicate effectively, and empathize with the perspectives of others. Emotional intelligence enables individuals to navigate conflicts with greater self-awareness, self-control, and social awareness, ultimately leading to more successful conflict resolution outcomes. By employing strategies such as communication, emotional intelligence, collaboration, and conflict coaching, individuals can address conflicts in a constructive and respectful manner, leading to sustainable resolutions that benefit all parties involved. Conflict resolution is not always easy, but with the right mindset, skills, and strategies, individuals can effectively manage conflicts and turn them into opportunities for growth and positive change.

- Teaching Healthy Communication in Disagreements

Communication is a fundamental aspect of human interaction, playing a crucial role in shaping relationships, resolving conflicts, and fostering understanding. In the context of disagreements, effective communication is especially important as it can determine the outcome of the interaction and impact the dynamics of the relationship. Teaching healthy communication in disagreements is essential for promoting constructive dialogue, managing conflicts, and building strong connections with others. By equipping individuals with the necessary skills and strategies to communicate effectively during disagreements, we can enhance their ability to navigate challenging situations, foster mutual respect, and cultivate positive interactions with others.

One key aspect of teaching healthy communication in disagreements is emphasizing the importance of active listening. Active listening involves paying attention to the speaker, understanding their perspective, and responding in a thoughtful and empathetic manner. By actively listening to the other person during a disagreement, individuals can demonstrate their willingness to understand the other's point of view, validate their feelings, and create a sense of mutual respect. Active listening can also help to de-escalate tensions, clarify misunderstandings, and facilitate productive dialogue, enabling individuals to work towards finding a resolution that is acceptable to both parties.

In addition to active listening, teaching healthy communication in disagreements also involves promoting assertiveness and conflict resolution skills. Assertiveness involves expressing one's thoughts, feelings, and needs in a clear and respectful manner, without infringing on the rights of others. By teaching individuals how to assert themselves in a non-confrontational way during disagreements, we can empower them to communicate their perspective effectively, set boundaries, and advocate for their own interests. Conflict resolution skills, on the other hand, involve the ability to negotiate, compromise, and find mutually agreeable solutions to disagreements. By helping individuals develop these skills, we can enable them to navigate conflicts in a constructive and collaborative manner, fostering understanding and cooperation among those involved.

Furthermore, teaching healthy communication in disagreements involves promoting emotional intelligence and self-awareness. Emotional intelligence is the ability to recognize, understand, and manage one's own emotions, as well as those of others. By cultivating emotional intelligence, individuals can navigate disagreements with empathy, self-control, and effective communication, leading to more positive outcomes and stronger relationships. Self-awareness, on the other hand, involves having a clear understanding of one's own thoughts, feelings, and behaviors, which can help individuals to communicate more authentically and responsively during disagreements. By encouraging individuals to develop these qualities, we can enhance their ability to communicate effectively, manage conflicts, and build trust and rapport with others.

Moreover, teaching healthy communication in disagreements also includes fostering a culture of respect, empathy, and inclusivity. Respect involves valuing the opinions, feelings, and perspectives of others, even if they differ from our own. By promoting respect in communication, we can create a safe and supportive environment for individuals to express themselves, share their thoughts, and engage in constructive dialogue. Empathy, on the other hand, involves understanding and sharing the feelings of others, which can help individuals to connect with others on a deeper level, build trust, and foster mutual understanding during disagreements. Inclusivity involves creating opportunities for all voices to be heard and valued, regardless of differences in opinion, background, or experience. By fostering a culture of respect, empathy, and inclusivity in communication, we can promote healthy interactions, foster collaboration, and strengthen relationships among individuals. By emphasizing active listening, assertiveness, conflict resolution skills, emotional intelligence, self-awareness, respect, empathy, and inclusivity, we can equip individuals with the necessary tools and strategies to communicate effectively during disagreements. Through these efforts, we can empower individuals to navigate challenging situations, manage conflicts, and foster positive interactions with others, ultimately leading to more harmonious relationships and productive outcomes. By prioritizing healthy communication in disagreements, we can create a culture of respect, understanding, and cooperation that benefits individuals, relationships, and communities as a whole.

- Navigating Generational and Cultural Differences

Generational and cultural differences play a significant role in shaping our understanding of the world and our interactions with others. As workplaces become increasingly diverse and multi-generational, it is essential to navigate these differences effectively to promote collaboration, understanding, and overall success. By acknowledging and respecting the unique perspectives and values of each generation and culture, we can create a more inclusive and harmonious environment for all.

One of the key challenges in navigating generational differences is the varying communication styles and preferences of different age groups. For example, Baby Boomers may prefer face-to-face communication and formal meetings, while Millennials and Gen Z individuals are more comfortable with digital communication and instant messaging. Understanding and adapting to these preferences can help bridge the gap between different generations and facilitate smoother communication and collaboration.

Cultural differences also play a significant role in shaping our interactions with others. Every culture has its own set of values, norms, and customs that influence how individuals perceive the world and behave in social situations. By recognizing and embracing cultural diversity, we can create a more inclusive and respectful environment that values the perspectives and contributions of people from different cultural backgrounds.

One of the key strategies for navigating generational and cultural differences is to practice empathy and active listening. By actively listening to others and putting ourselves in their shoes, we can gain a better understanding of their perspectives and experiences. This can help build trust and foster stronger relationships, leading to more effective communication and collaboration across generations and cultures.

Another important aspect of navigating generational and cultural differences is to promote diversity and inclusion within the workplace. By creating a culture that values and celebrates diversity, organizations can attract and retain talent from a wide range of backgrounds and experiences. This can lead to a more innovative and creative work environment that benefits from the unique perspectives and insights of individuals from different generations and cultural backgrounds. By acknowledging and respecting the unique perspectives and values of each generation and culture, we can create a more inclusive and harmonious environment that fosters collaboration, understanding, and success. By practicing empathy, active listening, and promoting diversity and inclusion, we can bridge the gap between different generations and cultures and create a more cohesive and productive workplace for all.

Chapter 15: Celebrating Milestones and Achievements

- RECOGNIZING YOUR DAUGHTER'S Accomplishments

Recognizing your daughter's accomplishments is an essential part of supporting her growth and development. By acknowledging and celebrating her achievements, you are not only boosting her confidence and self-esteem, but also motivating her to continue striving for success. It is crucial to show genuine interest in her accomplishments, no matter how big or small they may seem. Whether she wins an award at school, excels in sports, or achieves a personal goal, taking the time to recognize and praise her efforts will let her know that her hard work and dedication are valued.

One way to acknowledge your daughter's accomplishments is to praise her for her specific strengths and abilities. Instead of simply saying "good job," try to pinpoint what exactly she did well and why it was impressive. For example, if she excels in a particular subject at school, commend her for her dedication to studying and her ability to grasp challenging concepts. By recognizing the specific skills and qualities that led to her success, you are showing her that you truly understand and appreciate her hard work.

In addition to praising her accomplishments, it is also important to show your support and encouragement for her future goals and aspirations. Let your daughter know that you believe in her abilities and that you are there to support her in whatever she chooses to pursue. Encourage her to set new goals and challenge herself, and be there to offer guidance and assistance along the way. By creating a supportive and encouraging environment, you are helping to foster her self-confidence and determination to achieve even greater success in the future.

Another important aspect of recognizing your daughter's accomplishments is to celebrate her achievements in a meaningful way. This could involve organizing a small family gathering to commemorate her success, giving her a special gift as a token of your appreciation, or simply spending quality time together doing something she enjoys. By creating positive and memorable experiences around her accomplishments, you are reinforcing the value of hard work and perseverance, and creating lasting memories that she will cherish.

It is also crucial to remember that each individual has their own unique set of talents, strengths, and interests. As a parent, it is important to celebrate and recognize your daughter's accomplishments in a way that is meaningful to her. Take the time to understand what matters most to her and tailor your recognition efforts to align with her personal preferences and values. By showing genuine interest in her passions and accomplishments, you are not only acknowledging her achievements, but also demonstrating your love and support for who she is as an individual. By acknowledging her achievements, praising her strengths and abilities, and celebrating her success in a meaningful way, you are paving the way for her to reach her full potential and achieve great things in life. Remember to be genuine, supportive, and encouraging in your recognition efforts, and always strive to create a positive and nurturing environment for her to thrive. Your daughter's accomplishments are worth celebrating, and by acknowledging them, you are helping her build the confidence and resilience she needs to succeed in all aspects of her life.

- Marking Important Life Events

Marking important life events is a process that is deeply ingrained in human culture and society. From commemorating birthdays to celebrating graduations, marking these milestones allows us to reflect on our experiences, acknowledge our achievements, and connect with others. These events hold significant meaning for individuals and their communities, as they symbolize progress, growth, and moments of joy and accomplishment.

The act of marking important life events serves as a way for individuals to create lasting memories and establish a sense of identity and belonging. These milestones often serve as markers in the timeline of a person's life, helping to define who they are, where they come from, and where they are going. By acknowledging and celebrating these events, individuals are able to honor their past experiences, as well as look forward to what the future may hold.

In addition to the personal significance of marking important life events, these milestones also have broader societal implications. They serve as opportunities for communities to come together and show support for one another. Whether it be a wedding, a retirement party, or a baby shower, these events allow individuals to connect with others and forge relationships that can last a lifetime. They also provide a sense of unity and cohesion, as communities rally around those experiencing significant life changes.

One of the most common ways of marking important life events is through ceremonies or rituals. These rituals can take many different forms, depending on the event and cultural context. For example, a graduation ceremony may involve wearing a cap and gown, listening to speeches, and receiving a diploma. A wedding ceremony may include exchanging vows, exchanging rings, and sharing a first dance. These rituals help to formalize the event and make it more memorable for those involved.

Ceremonies and rituals are often accompanied by symbolic gestures or objects that hold special meaning. For example, a couple may exchange rings during a wedding ceremony to symbolize their commitment to each other. A graduation gown and cap may represent academic achievement and readiness to enter the next phase of life. These symbols serve as reminders of the significance of the event and help to reinforce its importance in the minds of those involved.

In addition to ceremonies and rituals, marking important life events can also involve the sharing of stories and memories. This can take the form of a toast at a wedding reception, a slideshow of a person's life at a retirement party, or a scrapbook of a child's first year of life. By sharing these stories and memories, individuals are able to reflect on the past, celebrate the present, and look forward to the future. This act of sharing helps to create a sense of connection and belonging among those present.

Another important aspect of marking important life events is the role of tradition and culture. Many of the rituals and ceremonies associated with these events have been passed down through generations and hold deep cultural significance. For example, a cultural coming-of-age ceremony may involve specific rituals and customs that have been practiced for centuries. These traditions help to reinforce a sense of community and shared identity among those participating in the event. These events allow individuals to reflect on their past, celebrate their achievements, and look forward to the future. Through ceremonies, rituals, and the sharing of stories and memories, individuals are able to create lasting connections with others and establish a sense of identity and belonging. This process of marking important life events not only benefits individuals on a personal level but also contributes to the cohesion and unity of communities as a whole.

- Encouraging Goal Setting and Growth

Encouraging goal setting and growth is an essential aspect of personal and professional development. Setting clear and achievable goals provides individuals with a sense of purpose and direction, while also serving as a roadmap for their future success. When individuals have goals to strive towards, they are more motivated and focused, which can lead to increased productivity and satisfaction in their lives. However, in order to effectively encourage goal setting and growth, it is important to understand the key principles and strategies that can help individuals set, pursue, and achieve their goals.

One of the first steps in encouraging goal setting and growth is to help individuals identify and define their goals. This involves taking the time to reflect on their values, interests, strengths, and aspirations in order to determine what they truly want to achieve. By setting clear and specific goals, individuals can create a vision for their future and establish a sense of purpose that drives them forward. It is important to emphasize the importance of setting both short-term and long-term goals, as this allows individuals to make progress towards their larger aspirations while also celebrating smaller victories along the way.

In addition to helping individuals define their goals, it is essential to provide them with the tools and resources they need to pursue and achieve them. This may involve setting deadlines, creating action plans, and breaking down larger goals into smaller, manageable tasks. By establishing a clear plan of action, individuals can stay organized and focused, which can help them overcome obstacles and stay on track towards their goals. Additionally, providing support and encouragement can also be beneficial in helping individuals stay motivated and committed to their goals, especially during challenging times.

Another important aspect of encouraging goal setting and growth is to foster a growth mindset in individuals. A growth mindset is the belief that abilities and intelligence can be developed through effort and perseverance. By promoting a growth mindset, individuals are more likely to view challenges as opportunities for growth and learning, rather than as setbacks. This can help individuals overcome obstacles, develop resilience, and ultimately achieve their goals. It is important to remind individuals that setbacks and failures are a natural part of the goal-setting process, and that they should not be discouraged by temporary setbacks or obstacles.

Creating a supportive and positive environment is also crucial in encouraging goal setting and growth. This involves providing individuals with feedback, praise, and recognition for their efforts and achievements. By acknowledging their progress and success, individuals are more likely to stay motivated and committed to their goals. It is also important to create a culture of accountability and transparency, where individuals feel comfortable sharing their goals and progress with others. This can help individuals stay focused and motivated, while also holding them accountable for their actions and decisions. By helping individuals set clear and achievable goals, providing them with the tools and resources they need to pursue their goals, fostering a growth mindset, and creating a supportive environment, we can empower individuals to reach their full potential and achieve their dreams. By emphasizing the importance of goal setting and growth, we can help individuals unlock their true potential and become the best version of themselves.

Chapter 16: Parenting Through Transitions and Changes

- SUPPORTING YOUR DAUGHTER Through Life Transitions

Life transitions can be challenging for anyone, but they can be particularly difficult for young girls navigating the complex journey from adolescence to adulthood. As a parent, it's important to provide support and guidance to your daughter during these transitions to help her navigate the changes and challenges that come with growing up. By understanding the unique experiences and needs of young girls, you can better equip yourself to be a supportive and nurturing presence in your daughter's life as she moves through these important milestones.

One of the key aspects of supporting your daughter through life transitions is to create a safe and open environment where she feels comfortable sharing her thoughts, feelings, and experiences. Adolescence can be a tumultuous time, filled with emotions and uncertainties, and it's important for your daughter to know that she can come to you for guidance and support. Be an active listener, offering your full attention and empathy as she talks about her fears, anxieties, and hopes for the future. By creating a space where she feels heard and understood, you can help her navigate the ups and downs of adolescence with confidence and resilience.

In addition to being a supportive listener, it's important to provide concrete tools and resources to help your daughter through life transitions. This could involve connecting her with mentors, therapists, or support groups that can offer guidance and support outside of the family unit. Encourage her to explore her interests and passions, whether through extracurricular activities, volunteer work, or creative pursuits. By fostering a sense of purpose and fulfillment in her life, you can help her build resilience and confidence as she navigates the challenges of growing up.

As your daughter moves through different life transitions, it's important to be a consistent and reliable presence in her life. This means showing up for important events, being available to offer guidance and support when needed, and consistently communicating your love and support for her. Even when things get tough, remind her that you believe in her abilities and strength to overcome challenges. By demonstrating your unwavering support and commitment to her well-being, you can help build her confidence and self-esteem as she transitions into adulthood.

It's also important to recognize that your daughter's journey through life transitions may be different from your own experiences. Every individual is unique, and it's important to approach each transition with an open mind and a willingness to learn and grow alongside your daughter. Be curious about her experiences, ask questions, and seek to understand her perspective on the changes and challenges she faces. By demonstrating a genuine interest in her journey and a willingness to learn from her experiences, you can strengthen your bond with your daughter and create a supportive and nurturing relationship that will endure through all of life's transitions. By creating a safe and open environment for her to share her thoughts and feelings, providing concrete tools and resources to help her navigate challenges, and being a consistent and reliable presence in her life, you can help your daughter build resilience and confidence as she moves through adolescence and into adulthood. Approach each transition with an open mind and a willingness to learn from her experiences, and you can strengthen your bond with your daughter and support her in becoming the confident and resilient woman she is meant to be.

- Navigating Puberty, College, and Beyond

Navigating the transition from adolescence through puberty, college, and beyond is a significant journey filled with numerous changes and challenges. Adolescence is a time of profound physical, emotional, and social transformation as individuals begin the process of transitioning into adulthood. Puberty, the period of sexual maturation, typically begins around the ages of 9-14 for girls and 10-17 for boys. During this time, adolescents experience rapid physical growth, hormonal fluctuations, and changes in their bodies as they develop secondary sexual characteristics.

Navigating puberty can be a daunting experience as individuals may struggle with body image issues, peer pressure, and a sense of identity. It is important for teenagers to receive support and guidance from trusted adults, such as parents, teachers, or healthcare providers, during this challenging time. Open communication and providing accurate information about puberty can help adolescents feel more comfortable and confident as they navigate this phase of development. Encouraging healthy habits, such as regular physical activity, proper nutrition, and good hygiene, can also support teens in managing the physical and emotional changes associated with puberty.

As adolescents transition into young adulthood, many face the next major milestone of attending college. College is a time of academic and personal growth, where individuals have the opportunity to pursue their interests, develop new friendships, and gain independence. However, the transition to college can also be a time of uncertainty and adjustment as students navigate new academic expectations, social dynamics, and living away from home for the first time.

To successfully navigate college, students can benefit from developing effective time management skills, seeking support from professors and academic advisors, and taking advantage of campus resources such as counseling services, tutoring centers, and career development programs. Building a strong support network of friends, mentors, and peers can also help students adjust to the demands of college life and feel connected to their campus community. Additionally, prioritizing self-care and wellness through activities such as exercise, mindfulness, and healthy eating can enhance students' overall well-being and academic success during their college years.

Beyond college, young adults continue to face a period of exploration and transition as they enter the workforce, pursue further education, or embark on independent living. The post-college years are a time of self-discovery and decision-making, as individuals navigate career choices, financial responsibilities, and personal relationships. It is important for young adults to continue nurturing their personal growth and development by setting goals, seeking mentorship, and engaging in lifelong learning opportunities.

Navigating the challenges of adulthood requires resilience, adaptability, and a willingness to seek support when needed. Building a strong personal and professional network, developing solid communication skills, and prioritizing self-care are essential components of navigating the complexities of adult life. By embracing change, taking risks, and learning from both successes and failures, individuals can navigate the transitions of puberty, college, and beyond with confidence and resilience.

- Adapting Your Parenting Style as Your Daughter Grows

Parenting is a dynamic and ever-evolving process that requires flexibility and adaptability. As children grow and develop, their needs, behaviors, and interests change, necessitating a shift in parenting strategies and approaches. This is particularly true when it comes to raising a daughter, as girls go through distinct stages of development that require parents to adjust their parenting style accordingly.

One of the key aspects of adapting your parenting style as your daughter grows is recognizing and respecting her individuality. Every child is unique, with their own personality, strengths, weaknesses, and preferences. As a parent, it is essential to acknowledge and honor your daughter's uniqueness, and tailor your parenting approach to suit her specific needs and temperament. This may require letting go of preconceived notions or expectations, and instead embracing and celebrating your daughter for who she is.

Another important aspect of adapting your parenting style as your daughter grows is staying informed and educated. Parenting is an ever-changing landscape, with new research, trends, and theories emerging all the time. It is crucial for parents to stay updated on the latest information and developments in child development, psychology, and parenting techniques. By staying informed, parents can make more informed decisions and choices when it comes to raising their daughters, ensuring that their parenting style is effective and appropriate for their daughter's changing needs.

As your daughter grows and matures, she will naturally gain more independence and autonomy. This can be both exciting and challenging for parents, as they navigate the delicate balance between providing guidance and support, while also allowing their daughter the freedom to make her own choices and decisions. It is important for parents to gradually loosen the reins as their daughter grows, giving her the space and opportunity to learn, grow, and develop her own sense of agency and responsibility. This may require parents to step back and resist the temptation to micromanage or control their daughter's every move, instead trusting in her ability to make good decisions and navigate the world on her own.

Communication is a crucial aspect of adapting your parenting style as your daughter grows. As children enter adolescence and young adulthood, they often become more reserved and private, making it challenging for parents to maintain open lines of communication. However, it is essential for parents to consistently communicate with their daughters, creating a safe and supportive environment where she feels comfortable sharing her thoughts, feelings, and experiences. This may require parents to actively listen, validate their daughter's emotions, and offer guidance and support without judgment or criticism. By fostering open and honest communication with their daughters, parents can strengthen their relationship and build trust, ensuring that they are able to effectively navigate the challenges and transitions of adolescence and young adulthood together.

Flexibility is another key component of adapting your parenting style as your daughter grows. As children grow and develop, their needs, interests, and priorities are likely to change, requiring parents to be flexible and willing to adjust their parenting approach accordingly. This may involve trying new strategies, exploring different approaches, and being open to feedback and input from your daughter. By remaining flexible and adaptive, parents can better meet their daughter's evolving needs and support her growth and development in a positive and effective way. By recognizing and respecting your daughter's individuality, staying informed and educated, allowing her more independence and autonomy, fostering open communication, and remaining flexible and adaptive, parents can effectively support their daughters as they navigate the challenges and transitions of adolescence and young adulthood. As parents, it is important to approach this process with an open heart and mind, and to remember that parenting is a journey that evolves and changes as your daughter grows and matures. By being present, supportive, and responsive to your daughter's evolving needs, you can help her thrive and succeed as she navigates the ups and downs of growing up.

Chapter 17: Cultivating Resilience and Grit

- INSTILLING PERSEVERANCE and Determination in Your Daughter

Instilling perseverance and determination in your daughter is a crucial aspect of her personal and professional development. These qualities are essential for navigating the challenges and obstacles that she may encounter throughout her life. By teaching your daughter to persevere in the face of adversity and to maintain a determined mindset, you are equipping her with the skills necessary to overcome obstacles and achieve her goals. In this essay, we will explore various strategies for instilling perseverance and determination in your daughter, as well as the benefits of cultivating these qualities in her early on.

One of the most effective ways to instill perseverance and determination in your daughter is to lead by example. Children often learn best by observing the behavior of their parents, so it is important to demonstrate these qualities in your own life. Show your daughter how you handle challenges and setbacks with grace and resilience. Share stories with her about times when you faced obstacles and persevered through them. By showing her that perseverance and determination are important values to you, she will be more likely to adopt them as her own.

Another important strategy for instilling perseverance and determination in your daughter is to encourage her to set goals for herself. Help her identify what she wants to achieve and work with her to create a plan for reaching those goals. Break down the steps needed to achieve her goals into manageable tasks, and celebrate her accomplishments along the way. By teaching your daughter to set goals and work towards them with determination, you are helping her build confidence in her abilities and develop a strong sense of perseverance.

It is also important to teach your daughter the importance of resilience. Resilience is the ability to bounce back from setbacks and failures, and it is a key component of perseverance. Encourage your daughter to view failures as learning opportunities rather than reasons to give up. Help her understand that setbacks are a natural part of life and that they can serve as valuable lessons for growth and development. By teaching your daughter to be resilient, you are helping her develop the inner strength and determination needed to overcome challenges and succeed in the face of adversity.

In addition to leading by example, setting goals, and fostering resilience, it is important to provide your daughter with support and encouragement as she works towards developing perseverance and determination. Offer words of encouragement when she faces challenges, and provide guidance and assistance when needed. Let her know that you believe in her abilities and that you are there to help her succeed. By creating a supportive and encouraging environment for your daughter, you are helping to instill in her the confidence and determination needed to persevere through difficult times.

It is also important to provide your daughter with opportunities to practice perseverance and determination in a variety of settings. Encourage her to try new things and step outside of her comfort zone. Whether it is participating in a challenging sports program, joining a club or organization, or pursuing a hobby that requires dedication and perseverance, exposing your daughter to new experiences will help her build the skills she needs to navigate the obstacles she may face in the future. By allowing her to practice perseverance and determination in different contexts, you are helping her develop the resilience and determination needed to overcome challenges in all areas of her life.

Lastly, it is important to celebrate your daughter's successes and acknowledge her efforts. Recognize her hard work and perseverance, and praise her for her accomplishments. By acknowledging her achievements, you are reinforcing the value of perseverance and determination in her mind. Celebrate her resilience in the face of challenges and praise her for her ability to maintain a determined mindset. By celebrating her successes, you are helping to build her confidence and motivation, and reinforcing the importance of perseverance and determination in her life. By leading by example, setting goals, fostering resilience, providing support and encouragement, offering opportunities for practice, and celebrating her successes, you can help your daughter develop the skills she needs to overcome obstacles and achieve her goals. By instilling in her the values of perseverance and determination early on, you are equipping her with the tools she needs to succeed in all areas of her life. With your guidance and support, your daughter can develop the inner strength and determination needed to navigate the challenges she may face and achieve her dreams.

- Teaching Resilience in the Face of Adversity

Resilience is a crucial skill that can help individuals navigate challenges and adversity with strength and determination. In the face of setbacks, failures, and hardships, resilience enables individuals to bounce back, adapt, and thrive in the face of adversity. Teaching resilience is an important aspect of education and personal development, as it equips individuals with the tools and strategies they need to cope with difficult situations and emerge stronger on the other side. By cultivating resilience in students, educators can empower them to face life's inevitable challenges with courage, perseverance, and positivity.

One key aspect of teaching resilience is fostering a growth mindset in students. A growth mindset is the belief that abilities and intelligence can be developed through effort, perseverance, and learning. By promoting a growth mindset in students, educators can help them understand that failure is not a permanent condition but an opportunity for growth and learning. Encouraging students to embrace challenges, learn from their mistakes, and persist in the face of setbacks can help them develop the resilience they need to overcome obstacles and succeed in the face of adversity.

Another important element of teaching resilience is helping students develop coping skills and strategies to manage stress, anxiety, and negative emotions. By teaching students how to identify their emotions, regulate their responses, and make positive choices in difficult situations, educators can help them build the resilience they need to navigate adversity with grace and confidence. Providing students with tools such as mindfulness techniques, positive self-talk, and stress management strategies can empower them to cope with setbacks and challenges in a healthy and effective way.

Additionally, teaching students the importance of self-care and self-compassion can help them cultivate resilience in the face of adversity. Encouraging students to prioritize their physical, emotional, and mental well-being can help them build the strength and resilience they need to overcome difficult circumstances. By teaching students how to practice self-care, set boundaries, and prioritize their needs, educators can empower them to navigate challenges with resilience, grace, and self-assurance.

Furthermore, fostering a sense of community and connection in the classroom can help students develop resilience in the face of adversity. By creating a supportive and inclusive learning environment where students feel safe, valued, and respected, educators can help students build the connections and relationships they need to thrive in the face of challenges. Encouraging collaboration, empathy, and teamwork can help students develop the social and emotional skills they need to navigate adversity with resilience, empathy, and compassion. By fostering a growth mindset, teaching coping skills and strategies, promoting self-care and self-compassion, and creating a sense of community and connection, educators can help students build the resilience they need to succeed in the face of adversity. Ultimately, by cultivating resilience in students, educators can help them develop the courage, perseverance, and positivity they need to overcome obstacles and thrive in the face of life's inevitable challenges.

- Building a Growth Mindset for Success

In today's fast-paced and constantly changing world, having a growth mindset is essential for achieving success. A growth mindset is the belief that your abilities and intelligence can be developed through hard work, perseverance, and learning from failures. This mindset is in contrast to a fixed mindset, where people believe that their abilities are static and cannot be changed. Research has shown that individuals with a growth mindset are more likely to take on challenges, persist in the face of setbacks, and ultimately achieve their goals.

One of the key principles of building a growth mindset is the idea that effort and learning are essential for growth and success. Embracing challenges and seeing failures as opportunities for growth are crucial elements of a growth mindset. When faced with a difficult task or setback, individuals with a growth mindset do not view it as a reflection of their abilities, but rather as a chance to learn and improve. They are willing to put in the effort to master new skills and overcome obstacles, knowing that their abilities can be developed with time and practice.

Another important aspect of building a growth mindset is fostering a love of learning and continuous improvement. People with a growth mindset are curious and open to new ideas, seeking out opportunities for growth and development. They actively seek feedback and are willing to embrace constructive criticism as a means of improving themselves. By cultivating a mindset of continuous learning and improvement, individuals can adapt to new challenges and opportunities in an ever-changing world.

In addition to effort and learning, cultivating resilience and perseverance are essential for building a growth mindset. Success rarely comes without setbacks, and individuals with a growth mindset understand that failure is a natural part of the learning process. They see setbacks as temporary obstacles that can be overcome with effort and perseverance. By viewing setbacks as opportunities for growth and learning, individuals with a growth mindset are able to bounce back from failure and continue moving forward towards their goals.

Developing a growth mindset is not always easy, as it requires a shift in thinking and behavior. It often involves challenging deeply held beliefs about intelligence, abilities, and success. However, with practice and dedication, anyone can develop a growth mindset and unlock their full potential. By embracing challenges, valuing effort and learning, and cultivating resilience and perseverance, individuals can build a foundation for success in both their personal and professional lives. By embracing challenges, valuing effort and learning, and cultivating resilience and perseverance, individuals can develop the mindset needed to overcome obstacles, adapt to new challenges, and ultimately achieve their goals. With dedication and practice, anyone can develop a growth mindset and unlock their full potential for success. By adopting a growth mindset, individuals can set themselves up for success in all areas of their lives, both personally and professionally.

Chapter 18: Conclusion

- REFLECTING ON YOUR Parenting Journey

Reflecting on your parenting journey can be a valuable exercise in understanding your growth, challenges, and successes as a parent. Parenting is a complex and dynamic role that requires constant adaptation and learning. By taking the time to reflect on your experiences as a parent, you can gain insights into your parenting style, values, and beliefs, as well as how they have evolved over time. This can help you make more informed decisions and improve your relationships with your children.

One important aspect of reflecting on your parenting journey is examining your own upbringing and how it has influenced your parenting style. Our own childhood experiences often shape the way we parent, whether consciously or unconsciously. By reflecting on your own upbringing, you can identify patterns and beliefs that you may be passing on to your own children. This self-awareness can help you make intentional choices about how you want to parent and break harmful cycles that may have been perpetuated from generation to generation.

Another key part of reflecting on your parenting journey is recognizing and acknowledging your strengths as a parent. It can be easy to focus on our shortcomings and areas where we feel we have fallen short, but taking the time to celebrate your successes and strengths as a parent is just as important. This can boost your confidence and self-esteem as a parent, as well as reinforce positive behaviors and patterns that you want to continue in your parenting journey.

Reflecting on your parenting journey can also help you identify areas for growth and improvement. Parenting is a lifelong learning process, and no one is perfect. By being open and honest with yourself about areas where you may need to grow or change, you can take proactive steps to become a more effective and supportive parent. This may involve seeking out support, resources, or guidance from other parents, professionals, or parenting experts to help you navigate the challenges and complexities of raising children.

One of the greatest benefits of reflecting on your parenting journey is the opportunity to deepen your connection with your children. By taking the time to understand your own experiences and beliefs as a parent, you can foster a more empathetic and compassionate relationship with your children. This can help you communicate more effectively, resolve conflicts peacefully, and create a loving and supportive environment for your children to thrive. Your willingness to reflect on your parenting journey and continuously learn and grow as a parent demonstrates to your children that you are committed to their well-being and development. By examining your own upbringing, celebrating your strengths, identifying areas for growth, and deepening your connection with your children, you can become a more intentional and effective parent. Parenting is a rewarding and challenging journey, and by engaging in reflective practices, you can cultivate a deeper understanding of yourself and your children, ultimately creating a more fulfilling and harmonious family dynamic.

- Looking Towards the Future

Looking towards the future, it is essential to consider the rapid advancements in technology and how they will continue to shape our world in the coming years. From artificial intelligence to blockchain technology, there are countless innovations on the horizon that have the potential to revolutionize industries and improve the quality of life for individuals around the globe. As we move forward, it is crucial for businesses and individuals alike to stay informed and adapt to these changes in order to remain competitive and thrive in an increasingly digital world.

One of the key trends to watch for in the future is the continued rise of artificial intelligence (AI) and machine learning. These technologies have already made a significant impact in a variety of sectors, from healthcare to finance to transportation. In the coming years, we can expect to see even greater advancements in AI as researchers and developers continue to push the boundaries of what is possible. This will have implications for businesses as well, as AI can help streamline operations, improve decision-making processes, and optimize efficiency in ways that were previously unimaginable.

Another area to keep an eye on is the development of blockchain technology. Originally created as the backbone of cryptocurrency, blockchain has since expanded into a wide range of applications, including supply chain management, voting systems, and healthcare records. As more industries adopt blockchain technology, we can expect to see increased transparency, security, and efficiency in various processes. This could have far-reaching implications for businesses looking to streamline operations and build trust with customers and partners.

In addition to technology, it is important to consider the impact of global trends and challenges on the future landscape. Climate change, for example, is a pressing issue that will continue to shape our world in the coming years. Businesses and individuals will need to adapt to the changing climate by embracing sustainable practices, reducing carbon emissions, and investing in renewable energy sources. This shift towards a more sustainable future will not only benefit the environment but also create new opportunities for innovation and growth.

Furthermore, the future of work is another area that will undergo significant changes in the years to come. As automation and AI continue to advance, the nature of work will evolve, with some traditional jobs being replaced by machines while others are created to support these new technologies. This will require individuals to acquire new skills and adapt to changing job requirements in order to remain competitive in the workforce. It will also necessitate a shift in mindset from companies, who will need to invest in training and retraining programs to ensure their employees are equipped to succeed in the digital age. By staying informed about emerging technologies, global trends, and changes in the workforce, businesses and individuals can position themselves for success in a rapidly evolving world. It is important to embrace innovation, adapt to new challenges, and seize opportunities for growth and development. By doing so, we can build a brighter future for ourselves and future generations.

- Embracing the Art of Understanding Your Daughter

Understanding your daughter is a complex and multifaceted task that requires patience, empathy, and a willingness to listen and learn. As parents, it is essential to recognize that each individual is unique and has their own set of beliefs, values, and experiences that shape who they are. By embracing the art of understanding your daughter, you can foster a strong and healthy relationship based on trust, mutual respect, and open communication.

One of the key aspects of understanding your daughter is acknowledging and respecting her individuality. Every person has their own unique personality, interests, and goals, and it is important to recognize and appreciate these differences in your daughter. By taking the time to really get to know her on a deep level, you can develop a greater understanding of her thoughts, feelings, and motivations. This will help you to better connect with her, build a stronger bond, and support her in achieving her full potential.

Another important aspect of understanding your daughter is being empathetic and sensitive to her emotions and experiences. Adolescence can be a challenging time for many young girls, as they navigate the complexities of self-identity, peer relationships, and societal expectations. It is crucial for parents to create a safe and supportive environment where their daughters feel heard, validated, and understood. By showing empathy and compassion, you can help your daughter feel supported and accepted, which can strengthen your relationship and foster a sense of trust and security.

Communication is a fundamental component of understanding your daughter. Effective communication involves not only talking but also listening actively and attentively. It is important to create opportunities for open and honest dialogue with your daughter, where she feels comfortable sharing her thoughts, feelings, and concerns. By engaging in conversations that are respectful, non-judgmental, and supportive, you can gain valuable insights into your daughter's inner world and deepen your understanding of her as a person. Listening without interrupting, offering guidance rather than criticism, and validating her emotions are all essential aspects of effective communication that can strengthen your relationship with your daughter.

In addition to communication, it is important to be observant and attentive to your daughter's nonverbal cues and body language. Often, young girls may struggle to express themselves verbally, but their body language can provide valuable insights into their emotions and needs. By paying attention to your daughter's nonverbal cues, you can better understand her moods, anxieties, and desires. This can help you to respond to her effectively, provide the support she needs, and create a nurturing and affirming environment for her to thrive.

Cultivating empathy and understanding for your daughter also involves recognizing and validating her emotions. Adolescence is a time of heightened emotional intensity, as girls navigate a range of feelings such as insecurity, sadness, anger, and joy. It is important for parents to acknowledge and validate their daughter's emotions, even if they may seem irrational or disproportionate. By recognizing and validating her feelings, you can help your daughter feel heard, understood, and supported, which can strengthen your relationship and build her emotional resilience.

Empowering your daughter to make independent decisions and express her opinions is another important aspect of understanding her. It is essential to recognize and respect your daughter's autonomy and agency, as she seeks to develop her own identity and assert her independence. By encouraging her to think for herself, make choices, and voice her opinions, you can help her cultivate self-confidence, self-esteem, and a sense of empowerment. This can enhance your daughter's sense of agency and self-worth, and enable her to navigate life's challenges with resilience and determination. By recognizing and respecting her individuality, empathizing with her emotions, communicating effectively, and validating her experiences, you can build a strong and healthy relationship with your daughter based on trust, respect, and mutual understanding. Through open dialogue, active listening, and empathetic communication, you can create a supportive and nurturing environment where your daughter feels valued, accepted, and empowered to be her authentic self. By embracing the art of understanding your daughter, you can strengthen your bond, foster her emotional well-being, and support her in achieving her full potential.